June

 S0-BDT-196

Joanus,

From one old pot to another

Happy Birthday!

Mark

A BOOK OF Pottery

From Mud Into Immortality

By Henry Varnum Poor

AN ARTIST SEES ALASKA

Bowl with reducing reds, by H. V. Poor

A BOOK OF Pottery

From Mud Into Immortality

BY

HENRY VARNUM POOR

PRENTICE-HALL, INC.

Englewood Cliffs, N.J.

© 1958 by HENRY VARNUM POOR

All rights reserved, including the right to reproduce this book, or any portions thereof, in any form, except for the inclusion of brief quotations in a review.

Library of Congress Catalog Card Number 58-11375

Printed in the United States of America

08007

In a year of Outer Space and Sputniks

this book is dedicated to E A R T H

FOREWORD

I SHOULD BE PLEASED if the practical and "how to do it" parts of this book made pottery an "anyone can do it" craft, for it is precisely in that self-taught tradition that I started, and have now for thirty-six years continued in the making of pottery. But not as a spare time or casual avocation. From the beginning it was a twelve-hours-a-day job by which I earned my living to the complete exclusion, during the first ten years, of any serious painting. But not of drawing. I drew constantly the birds, beasts, flowers, fruits, all the things around me, and was constantly occupied with their adaptation to ceramic design. And some analysis of this second aspect of pottery making, which involves a way of life, is the prime reason for the writing of this book.

—HENRY VARNUM POOR

Table of Contents

[9]

List of Illustrations

COLOR PLATES

HALFTONE ILLUSTRATIONS

LINE DRAWINGS IN THE TEXT

A BOOK OF Pottery

From Mud Into Immortality

CHAPTER ONE

From Mud Into Immortality

Earth I am, it is most true
Disdain me not, for so are you.
—MOTTO FROM EARLY
ENGLISH PLATE

AS ROCK BROKE UP INTO SAND, and sand disintegrated into clay or dirt, or mud, the live surface of the globe came into being. How organic life began no one knows, but it sprang most directly from mud, and is most dependent on mud for its continued existence. The miracle of life and growth involves air, water, and earth, all activated by heat, and of these the tangible element of earth is most closely bound up with the life of man.

From the beginning man knew that he came from earth and returned to earth. If you, the reader of this book, have no memories of wading through puddles after a rain and the delight of feeling soft mud oozing up between your bare toes, then you are not likely to become a potter—unless these memories go back further than your conscious self. They are your inescapable birthright. They are the reason for the constant recurrence of and return to primitivism in all the arts. They are the reason for the universality of symbols. They are the reason that a life of the imagination can inform you of things beyond your experience and make even the sterile environment of the city-dweller tolerable.

One of the primary instincts of man is to leave a record of himself. "Kilroy was here," the record of the rambling hobo scratched on railroad bridges, embankments and along highways, is a survival of the primitive in us. It is a form of communication and yearning as lonely and inarticulate as the peeing of a dog against every post where he smells his kind. And for purposes of record, clay or mud was ever present to early man. He could shape it, he could scratch into it and leave impressions, he could use it as paint with which to color harder substances or draw on them. It was the most delectable, the most obedient, the most inviting of all substances that came to the hand.

And the discovery of how clay—this soft, plastic, impressionable substance—was transformed by heat back into the hard durable rock from which it came, must have been made along with the earliest use of fire. The record of early man in clay transmuted by fire, the record of the objects he made and the aspirations he had—these are the most universal of all records.

And mud has preserved the most perfect records of life that existed before man. The delicate tracery of leaves, of ferns, of fragile forms long vanished are preserved in shale as vividly as are the specimens that lie pressed between the blotters of a botanist's book. Of all inorganic substances, clay most approaches the organic; it seems almost to contain in itself the breath of life. And it is the host that holds loam, the soluble salts, and all the other elements that support vegetation.

Plasticity

It is the mysterious quality of plasticity that makes clay so alive, so responsive. Plasticity is like a life force in itself, an extension of every
impulse, every touch. Dreams and thoughts become tangible through
this quality. And strangely enough, plasticity defies exact explanation.
A great deal has been written about it, and much scientific study devoted to it, but the basis for the live molecular attraction that makes
plasticity seems to elude analysis. It does not lie in the impalpable fineness of the individual particles that compose it, for sand or rock or any
of the basic constituents of clay can be ground mechanically to the same
fineness, but the resulting paste is lifeless.

Clays

The term clay is actually a relative term, since clay may be largely sand
and since even a loamy, friable soil may hold much clay. It is the product
of the decomposition of rock, but there is such a wide variety in the
chemical composition of various clays and in their other characteristics
that for the practical purposes of a potter, clay could be defined as a
plastic earth which becomes permanently hard when subjected to heat.

Briefly, clays are aluminum silicate—the product of the decomposition of feldspathic rock.

When clays occur in beds, at their source they are white, are not
very plastic or widely distributed, and are called china clay or kaolin.
They are the clays from which china and porcelain ware are made, and
they require high temperatures to mature them. These are *primary*
clays.

The *secondary* clays are sedimentary deposits of the primary clays, which often have been carried far from their source and have picked up many impurities, mainly iron, which color them red or tan or gray. The action of the water and the addition of the impurities have rendered them plastic and more fusible. They are widely distributed over the earth and occur either in beds, often free from gravel and organic matter, or are present in the soil almost everywhere.

From the land back of my pottery in Rockland County, New York, I dug earth from about six inches below the surface to get it fairly free from roots, leaf mould, and other obvious organic substances. It was a yellow, rather sandy soil, not clay-like or plastic in feeling. I put some of it through a $\frac{1}{4}$-inch mesh sieve and measured out one gallon of this earth which had been separated from its biggest pebbles. This gallon of earth I stirred into three gallons of water, making a thin, yellow soup, which I poured through a $\frac{1}{8}$-inch sieve. About one pint of pebbles remained on the sieve. On a $\frac{1}{16}$-inch mesh sieve rather more than a pint of sharp clean sand remained. Through a forty-mesh sieve about half of the remaining soup passed. This I allowed to settle overnight; then I siphoned off the clear water and poured the heavy creamy remainder into a plaster bat. This process resulted in a clay that was plastic enough to be thrown into simple forms on the wheel. At cone 05 it made a pleasant, sandy-textured, terra-cotta-red body, perfectly strong and durable. It was rich and glossy under a simple raw glaze. It would make fine kitchen casseroles for baking.

I am not a geologist, nor am I interested in mapping out clay distribution, but wherever I drive and find clay exposed in roadside cuts I gather it, carry it home and, when I find time, make some simple bowls. Then in my imagination I can see the beautiful and useful things which could come from that region, could uniquely characterize the place through its deviations from the accepted and standardized products of industrial ceramic plants. This sort of regionalism we have unfortunately left behind, and in doing so have lost more than we have gained. Who with a sense of taste would not gladly exchange our packaged and universally marketed bread, properly "vitamin enriched," for the loaves from ovens of any French or Italian town, made from the villagers' own wheat?

What I have just said makes me realize early in the writing of this book that much of what I want to say will be destructive, or will seem destructive, to the reader who looks only for affirmations of what *is*, who thirsts for knowledge, who wants to know *how* to do things. The *how* to do things interests me deeply, but not the purely technical "know-how" on which we Americans pride ourselves.

The "how to do," which starts with the impulse and traces the motivation and direction which this urge to do must or should follow, is, I believe, of vast importance to us. Certainly it is immensely important in analyzing or pointing a meaningful direction which may help us to rewarding and significant work. So, as you who have read so far may gather, this is an anti-technical book. As in painting, I am very little interested in how you put on the paint—I think that for anyone with the necessary gift as a starting point, that easily solves itself when you become fully aware of what you want to do.

So in using clay as a medium, whether for making pots or ceramic sculpture or modelled plaques or whatnot, the know-how which I want to talk about will be always on a rule-of-thumb, skill-of-hand, or primitive trial-and-error basis, rather than on one proceeding from a knowledge of chemistry, or exact technical processes—which knowledge I do not have. Although I have often regretted the lack of this knowledge, I have become more convinced through the years that this lack may have been an asset.

If, from the point of view of my reader, this attitude seems perverse, I wish to explain. I think that not only our present day art, including that of ceramics, but our whole present day civilization is engaged in a life and death struggle with the forces of technique, of mass production, of conformity in all that surrounds us physically, and that inevitably works its way into our spiritual and intellectual life and determines our creative life. That machine and mass production produces the leisure by which our inner life can soar to new heights is, I think, a tragic fallacy more recognized with the passing of every year.

[21]

Art is an expression of each person's rediscovery of the universe. To produce a living and vital art this discovery must begin close to the beginning, or the result is only a synthetic art. The beginning for pottery is clay.

> Earth I am, it is most true
> Disdain me not, for so are you.

This motto on an old English plate expresses the spirit which motivated a whole national period of potmaking in England. And although later English ceramic products, such as Wedgwood, Toft, Staffordshire, Chelsea, and Bow, became famous the world over for perfection of technique and distinctive style, this work never soared so high into realms of pure and expressive form as did the rugged pots of those early English potters.

So the love of clay, through as personal an experience as may still be possible in this nervous, rushing, industrialized, present day America, is the most important starting point for everyone who has the urge to make pottery. This is why I tell of digging it up in my own back yard. I like to call it mud to emphasize its universality and to emphasize that the most common may be the richest materials from which to make rare and beautiful objects. You can go to a supply house and buy clay, dug, refined, tested, and ready for use. You will know that thousands of others are using that same clay, and that it is safe; and if this is comforting, reflect too that thousands of others in their standardized kilns are going to turn out very much the same standardized product as you are. Then ask yourself, do you really want to do this? If the answer is no, please explore your own neighborhood for beds of clay, dig it, and subject yourself to the experience of *knowing* that it is earth and not a synthetic paste or powder made up of God knows what.

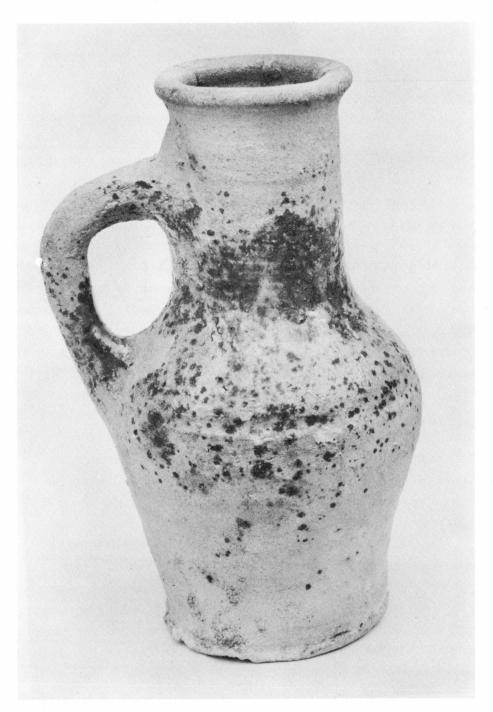

Early English pot (Courtesy of THE METROPOLITAN MUSEUM OF ART)

Preparing Clay

I will assume that you have found and dug some clay, so I will tell you the simplest way to prepare it for use. (If you have bought it from a shop, it is ready for use, so I have nothing to say to you now, though later I may be able to offer helpful suggestions as to how to use it.)

In some clay beds, the deposits are so clean and uniform that no screening is necessary. But even so, if the clay is tough and leathery it is very hard to make it take up the necessary amount of water to render it evenly plastic enough for use. It is easier to let it get completely dry and start from there. So spread it out in the sun or in a dry place. Then, when it is completely dry, break it up with a hammer or a paddle so it will go through a ¼-inch sieve; fill a pail three-quarters full of this dry broken clay and pour water over it, flooding it completely. It takes up water immediately, and if you plunge your arm in to the bottom, stirring it and seeing that water has got evenly through the whole mass, within an hour of soaking you will have a smooth thin slip which you can pour now through a 20 or, say, window-screen size mesh. Doing this you will have caught the occasional pebble which even in a very clean native clay might later turn up in the thin wall of a piece you are throwing, or if it went undetected into the kiln, might expand and shale off a piece of your pot.

Let this slip stand a few hours and you can pour or siphon off the clear water at the top. Pour the remaining thick slip onto plaster bats or into large bowls made of plaster which quickly absorb the water until the slip stiffens, and separates itself from the plaster. Then you can pick it up and handle it as a lump of clay. In this form you can prepare and store as much clay as you want in any covered container. It improves with age, but it is better to keep it more soft and wet than you care to use it, since it is much easier to stiffen by repeated cutting and throwing onto a plaster bat than it is to soften it once it has become too stiff.

[24]

Short clay is clay that is too sandy and is inclined to crumble at the edges when you press it between your fingers. *Fat* clay is clay that is jelly-like. It seems very plastic, but it has a tendency to settle back and disappoint you by not holding the shape you have put it into, and it shrinks and becomes distorted in drying.

If you want to change the composition of your clay by mixing with other clays to correct its being too fat or too short; or if you want to add sand or grog to make a better modelling clay, you can do it most easily while your clay is in slip form. Then whatever you have added will be evenly distributed through the whole mass.

Obviously, the best clay for both potting or modelling is one that has a minimum shrinkage and is plastic but holds strongly the shape you put it into.

In preparing clay for use either in building or modelling or tile making, and most particularly for throwing on the wheel, two things are of first importance. First, the ball of clay you start with should be absolutely uniform in hardness—no hard and soft lumps. Second, it should be free from imprisoned air bubbles. The simplest way to insure both of these is to cut your clay batch repeatedly over a wire, and slam the two halves violently down on a plaster slab, one on top of the other. This is called *wedging*, and the following diagram shows the simplest way to do it.

A ball of clay weighing about twelve pounds—say about seven inches in diameter—is good to handle easily without tiring. If you're big and strong, it can be bigger; if you are small and delicate, it can be smaller.

Lay the ball on the plaster slab and under the slanting wire. Then with one arm on each side of the wire, hold the ball between your hands and bring them sharply up, cutting the clay in half as it rises against the wire. Then slam each half sharply down, one on each side of the wire, turning the second half as you throw it so that the two cut sides face away from each other. This soon becomes a rhythmic and easy motion which after ten minutes of pleasant exercise will give you a ball of clay free from bubbles, smooth, and even in texture.

This clay now is ready for use. It is the most soft and impressionable of all materials, but you must love it and respect it before it will come alive in your hands.

CHAPTER TWO

Images and Objects

THE URGE TO MAKE IMAGES was as basic in primitive man as the urge to make "things" or objects. Images and objects were twin expressions of much the same creative urge, and very often and very naturally the man of exceptional skill in one was also good at the other. Tools, utensils of all kinds, primitive artifacts of exceptional skill and refinement of form, often are decorated with and even become, through imaginative enrichment, beautiful images. Images are less earthbound than objects, more part of man's desire to communicate, more allied to song and dance and to picture writing, which came out of images through the development of symbols for things. Objects, of course, were for use; but the urge to make them beautiful too was as active as the urge to communicate, and their beauty in itself became a communication.

From their *use* side came science—the gathering of knowledge about how to make them with the most perfect materials, how to make them most completely adapted to their use, and how to make them with greatest perfection. So from the beginning science and art have had much the same relation to each other that they have today—undoubtedly very much bound up together, seeming like twins in one way, but just as often seeming like unrelated opposites. The great and fundamental separation came with the development of the machine and the industrial age—the rapid development of science. This separated the things we live with—all the ordinary *use* objects of our daily life—from any human and communicated warmth. As a result science and the products of science quickly assumed an overpowering role in our lives, separating the tangible and material forces and contacts from the spiritual, the living and human, and tragically weakening the unity and completeness of life out of which the most richly creative epochs had come in the past.

Men and Materials

Every work of art is a fusion of Man, his Spirit, and the stuff from which the thing is made. Sometimes there is conflict, sometimes there seems to be perfect accord between these two; but the evidence of conflict does not necessarily negate the eloquence of the final work. The evident sense of struggle may be part of its eloquence.

The ratio of the parts in this duality is very shifting. The material can be all important; or the spirit, the intention of the creator, can completely swamp the material. I think the most eloquent works of art are those in which you are always conscious of both. In the greatest enjoyment of poetry you are conscious of the words. In music you distinguish the instruments. Architecture is inseparable from the

Pottery from Costa Rica (Courtesy of THE AMERICAN MUSEUM OF NATURAL HISTORY)

basic materials of stone, wood, and metal. When synthetic materials entirely replace these, you have a new concept of architecture—"enclosed space," which is no longer architecture but has become Le Corbusier's "Machine for Living," in which only human machines can be content to live.

Through the history of painting and sculpture there has been a constant shifting of emphasis between the two parts in this dual structure. Complete mastery or subordination of material generally marks the end of a movement, or an epoch; a fresh vision or movement comes largely through or is certainly accompanied by a return to, or a new discovery of, the beauty of materials.

Through the centuries, painting travelled to a point where the illusion became perfect. The paint which produced the illusion became nothing, and men like Rembrandt and Courbet, who grew more and more to love thick, sensuous, heavy pigment, were thought to be clumsy technicians. Then, through the Impressionists, paint as a substance and pigment as a material began to play a leading part in all the various modern movements which revitalized painting.

Sculpture followed the same course. From the complete mastery of marble represented in Michelangelo's *Pietà,* where could a sculptor go? Only to simpler forms in which the material began to play again an increasingly important part. Brancusi's whole art consists of an attempt to find the spirit inherent in a material, and other present day sculpture is excessively preoccupied with material. However, when the material like sheet metal or even "found" scraps of tools and machines is already pre-fabricated and is manipulated through the remote control of a blow torch, the spirit which emerges is likely to be a rather bastard hybrid. Even so it is better than a stillborn imitation.

On the rare occasion of the emergence of a really new material or new method such as that of steel and concrete in building, new vitality appears; but all valid revivals or rebirths in art are, I think, accompanied by fresh exploration into the uses of material. Often this revival is simply a return, for art is a sea with rising and falling tides, not a river moving always ahead.

[30]

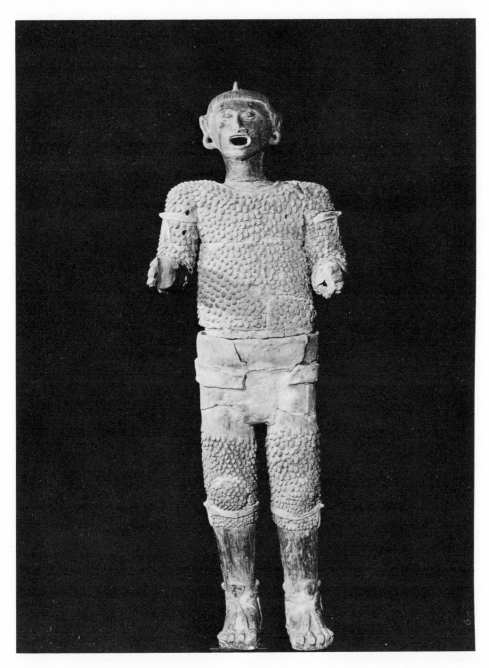

Terra cotta figure representing the God Xipe Totec, found in a cave near Texcoco, Mexico (Courtesy of THE AMERICAN MUSEUM OF NATURAL HISTORY)

[31]

In art there is no perfection, nor even a universal image of perfection. Individuals have set images of perfection for themselves, but the images come to an end with that individual. And wherever an image of perfection did dominate the whole production of a people or a school, the result was a sterility like that of the late Greek periods, as shown both in their sculpture and their pottery. Art is continually reborn and revivified and can build on inherited knowledge and tradition only to a limited extent. Even the painting of Cézanne, which seemed so reasonable, so reasoned, so much a ladder leading to greater perfection, has not truly served as a ladder, for what was continued in its image became dead.

In returning to the warm beauty of marble where it is common and lies scattered over the hillsides or is built into fences as in Greece or Italy or Vermont, and is weathered by the rain and made golden by the sun, a sculptor finds that the cold white perfection of Michelangelo's *Pietà* has entirely subdued and throttled these warm marble qualities. But as he simplifies his forms and finds new vitality in the marble, he goes forward by going back to the primitive Kouri—those blocks of stone, half nervous spirit, half beautiful marble—perhaps the most eloquent of all Greek sculpture.

Science, on the other hand, sets a goal—the perfection of knowledge, the all-knowing. The oceanographer hopes eventually to find out all there is to know about the floor of the ocean. The chemist hopes to make the perfect substance. The perfect porcelain is the goal of the industrial porcelain factory.

Thus the so-called fine arts must always stay close to the crafts, where obviously the material is of first importance. Perhaps the distinction between fine arts and applied arts could be made on some rough ratio between spirit and material. Certainly much painting and sculpture is pure exercise in craftsmanship, while many simple objects of clay and wood and metal reveal the most lofty spirit.

Pottery is earth begotten; but the most powerful of all catalysts, heat, frees it from being earthbound. After the potter has done his best with his material, heat works its miracles until the results far transcend the creator. I know of no other art, no other technique, where this is true. Heat and growth and equally miraculous forces have conspired to produce the stone and wood, metals and colors that are the materials of all the arts. When man has done his best with them, he carefully protects the result. Only the potter trusts his completed work to God or the Devil for its final perfection or destruction.

In the arts of all primitive people there are astonishing similarities, and particularly so in pottery. If the way of life and the materials at hand were in close correspondence, then the natives of the Congo, the Indians of Mexico and Peru, the early Cretans and Persians, and the prehistoric Chinese, all did work that was much more alike, much more akin in both outward form and inner spirit, than is the work of two different artists who might be showing simultaneously in New York's 57th Street galleries today, although these two painters might be of the same age, live in the same building, read the same books and newspapers and buy their paint and canvas from the same shop. The likenesses in work separated by thousands of years and by unknown continents certainly show that men were so alike in physical and spiritual needs that they evolved the same forms and the same decorations and much the same symbolic imagery.

The present day *differences* result from many and complicated disruptive forces. Conformity in our lives leads to a false emphasis upon differences and originality as an assertion of freedom. From an imagined retrospective view of 3,000 years hence, similarities which now we do not see will probably appear much greater. At any rate, the paintings will be on much the same canvas and with much the same paints and will have been painted with much the same self-conscious motivation, the same lack of unity with our everyday life. But I don't think 3,000 years can bring forward much similarity between a realistically modelled marble nude and a welded abstract construction in sheet iron, which might today be included in the same exhibition of Contemporary Art.

What Is Our Tradition?

A good design is a living thing. It is not invented. It is evolved out of a way of life, but even so its variations are infinite and unpredictable. The grasshopper, the katydid, the giraffe are all leaf-eating creatures, but strange and beautifully unpredictable. The artist, the designer, is a maker of images, images that are evolved from the living creatures around him, made from the materials which he has to use and governed by his understanding of organic living form.

In our present day America many of the formalized images that became, for a particular time and place, universally recognized symbols no longer are valid. The way of life and the techniques, the limited and characteristic materials, that led to their evolution have vanished. This expression common to a people is tradition, a whole race speaking with a power beyond any individual. The great cultures of the world, and also the most universally eloquent artists, have been the product of and part of a tradition. Without this common language you have Babel, and men shouting in strange tongues trying to be understood through the loudness of their voices and the assertiveness of their styles.

In the arts based on clay transmuted by fire—the ceramic arts —the materials at hand and the techniques involved have played a leading part in forming tradition. The Chinese had kaolin and white burning clays and feldspar, and what they did with these became a tradition that profoundly influenced the art of ceramics throughout the world. The Etruscans knew and loved their red clay, the slippery mud that oozed up between their bare toes; and they learned to build images of it and depict their whole life through it. They were laid away in caskets made of it, with images of themselves lying in immortal state over their own mortal flesh. They delighted in the mystery of firing this red mud and manipulating the fire to get a glossy black—the Bucchero ware which still defies science to duplicate it. So they made a terra cotta civilization. The Persians, imitating the Chinese whiteware, used their own coarse sandy clays overlaid with a white slip, and decorated their pots with such brilliance under fat soda and potash glazes that they give us a delight of an entirely different sort. Italian and Moorish majolica, Delft enameled ware, early English earthenware and stoneware and slipware—all the ceramic things we most love—speak of a time, a place, a people, a way of life.

For us, now, what is our tradition? In our homes, as much as we can, we live with things we love from all places and all times. If we cannot own them (and generally we cannot), we gloat over them as reproduced in books, and in museums. We inherit all traditions and are part of what? When we go to buy cups and plates and bowls—the things we use and spend our lives with, the common things—we get sanitary, cold, mechanically perfect machine-made objects, perhaps well designed by some efficient industrial designer. Must we accept this as our tradition? In all honesty it *is* the American tradition in ceramics—good, even perfect, sanitary hotel china. This is the voice of our way of life, and it speaks in precise, cold, impersonal tones of factories, machines and mass production.

We must face the fact that this is our common voice, and if we are not in tune and are not content to be in tune, our problem becomes one of finding quiet and detachment to develop and perfect our own little voices. And how escape the self-conscious individualism, the unhealthy too-long-indulged introspection, which has become the role of the artist? Sophisticated primitivism is a very tricky role for the artist to play in his attempt to recapture the singleness of other simpler civilizations. In pottery, the return must be made through closer, warmer touch with our materials. But in our shops we have *all* materials; in our schools and textbooks and workshops we have command of *all* techniques. We can buy any and all perfect glazes to fit any perfect body, put them into an electric kiln, turn a switch, and fire them to exactly the right temperature. So all that is lacking is good design and there are many books and teachers to tell what good design is—so, where is the perfect pottery?

Pot from Mangbetu, Africa
(*Courtesy of* THE AMERICAN
MUSEUM OF NATURAL HISTORY)

It would seem that the living quality of a piece of pottery hangs on a delicate balance. Technical perfection cannot give life to dead forms and dry design. Only love can create a living thing; knowledge is not enough. To know exactly how a clay acts and what its qualities are is not the same by any means as loving it into life and nursing it through the mysteries and uncertainties of firing.

To make your own valid tradition I think you must have, above all, the hardihood to establish and maintain a way of life, and this must involve a closer, warmer relation to your materials and, as an image maker, a life lived in close contact with the things from which you want to evolve symbols and images. The bird you may evolve to fit a pot may be very like a Persian bird; but if you have arrived at it through your own knowledge of birds, through your own drawings and attempts

[36]

to summarize what you know and see, its differences from an adapted Persian bird mark the difference between something trite and something alive. *Character,* a quality beyond words or analysis, is the very first quality in good design, and any design that sacrifices character to any imagined rightness, any conformity to law, is no longer good design.

And for your clay, character again is much more important than any supposed perfection. Clays are like wines, in that part of their flavor comes from the winemaker's knowledge of the hillsides and vineyards that grew the grapes. So if you can't dig clay in your own back yard, try to get it locally. It does not have to be perfect—its limitations and imperfections may help you. As for techniques, try to master one and use it with invention and skill; you may find that it will keep you going all your life.

The simplicity we need is not the ineptness of amateurism. It is a technical simplicity which puts the chief emphasis upon fine form, skilled craftsmanship, and living, expressive design. Of the accumulation of the art of all ages with which we live, the multiplicity of techniques and materials, you must be content to leave a great deal alone. It will be a long time, perhaps never again, before this complex pattern

White painted Kylix from Cyprus (c. 750-500 B.C.), modelled into the face of a monkey (Courtesy of THE METROPOLITAN MUSEUM OF ART)

Pottery from Costa Rica (*Courtesy of* THE AMERICAN MUSEUM OF NATURAL HISTORY)

Pottery figures from Western Mexico. Small dogs like this are still found in the state of Colima, Mexico (*Courtesy of* THE AMERICAN MUSEUM OF NATURAL HISTORY)

[38]

of life becomes clear and single. The directions you follow must be your own, and the work you do may be incomplete and fragmentary. But it will give you endless pleasure in doing, and it may live, if you can be true to your own lump of clay and to the fire that makes it immortal.

In preparing this book, and going back after a lapse of years to renew my acquaintance with the pottery in our museums, I found myself most enchanted by, most drawn to, work from what corresponds to the so-called Bronze Age in Europe and the East, around 3000 B.C. On our continent, work of corresponding cultures came much later, but the clay objects of early Peruvian, Central American, and Western Mexican peoples closely resemble in technical methods and human qualities the work of early Egyptians, Assyrians, and Chinese.

The wealth of beautiful work from our own continent gave me a chauvinistic pleasure and moved me to dream of how these cultures might have influenced the world if they had not been violently snuffed out through conquest or climatic changes. That they would have produced any finer works of art I do not believe, for I think the finest work in all these cultures—near Eastern, Oriental, or American—came at the period of lively fresh invention, before either form or decoration became formalized and repetitive and before technical processes became of first importance. The later periods are rich in "objets d'art"—*objects* of art (Chinese porcelains, for instance)—while the earlier things can truly be called *works* of art: fresh, expressive masterpieces.

You as an individual potter may call yourself a descendant of, or may belong to the family and the live tradition of, any time and place and way of working that speaks most directly and clearly to you. How direct and productive that attachment, that spiritual alignment, may be is hard to say. The trouble is that it may be and probably is largely spiritual and temperamental, and weak in direct material attachment and continuity of methods and materials. To many potters, particularly those fascinated by high temperatures and attracted by technical problems, Chinese porcelains are the apex, the lure that leads them on. Your choice is wide, but do not think that in a craft or art as rich in tradition as that of pottery you can be an entirely unattached maverick. That is affectation.

For myself, going back to look at the free, lively, unglazed little cup which was in a way my starting point in pottery making, I found the fingerprints of that Stone Age Cretan who, 3,000 years ago, threw it and lifted it from his wheel and fired it in his smoky flame. The cup was still as fresh as on the day he made it, and this miracle of a live and fluid substance made enduring by fire, this direct communication through the touch of a hand, is one of the most endearing things in the profession—or the art—of pottery making.

CHAPTER THREE

The Hand of the Potter and the Origin of Style

MANY OF THE IDEALS which I held in my youth have gone by the board as I've lived through thirty-seven years of pottery making. Some were abandoned because I replaced them with what I felt were better ideals, but "better" means, when I examine it, just more practical or possible. Very seldom could you justly call the new ideals "higher." The beginning of everything is the time for high ideals and a "no compromise" spirit, and I have found that I greatly value good intentions. A man full of good intentions, but also full of frailties, is a better, more endearing friend than the "always right," salt-of-the-earth variety.

In the world's painting great names dominate; and young painters love, say, Giotto, Rembrandt, Goya, Matisse. But in ceramics you love the products of a race, a period, a region; and the individual creators are very properly anonymous.

All the great traditions were reflections of a way of life and seldom involved a conscious choice. The work was what it was because the needs and taste of the people of a certain place, and the materials native to or available in that place, determined its character.

The Chinese were blessed with a wealth of clays that led them into the refinements of porcelain. The Persians tried for the same whiteness, but having only a sandy clay, developed their white slip. The Etruscans, surrounded with a plastic red clay, expressed their whole life in terra cotta.

None of these potters faced the most difficult problem which faces you and me in America today: with *all* materials, *all* techniques, *all* varieties of taste to choose from, but no immediate, specific and crying need to be filled, what are we going to do? How are we going to work? What will be our tradition? To what family of potters will we belong?

One of my great loves when I started doing pottery was Persian pottery, and the technique of working on a white slip, which I took from the Persians, has remained, through various modifications, my greatest love. It offers the freest and richest medium of expression for informal draughtmanship and pictorial decoration; and since I was most in love with painting and drawing, I started doing pottery for the pleasure of decorating it.

In the pottery of the Persians it is the universality of the tradition, the very commonness of the work, which plays an essential part in forming its fresh, vigorous character. This attitude toward their work on the part of the potters charmed me. I valued the three scars of the stilts on even the most beautiful plates and bowls, showing they were stacked in tiers, as a finer trade mark than an artist's signature. My first ambition was to produce beautiful, common, and anonymous ware and to sell it cheaply. I wanted to flood the market with it so that people would rush to buy, knowing only that it came from "that pottery up the Hudson near Haverstraw." The body of this ware would be that blue clay of the Hudson Valley, where were made the common red bricks with which early New York City was built.

This ideal has been abandoned, and largely through economic pressure—the poison that destroys more ideals than any other killer. I had named my house and pottery "Crowhouse"; had cut out a stamp for a trade mark. I never signed my work, but with my first venture into taking orders by the dozens from the Belle Maison Gallery at Wanamaker's, I realized I must either become a small factory and have helpers, or stick to my solitude and ask higher prices. The latter is what happened.

But that original ideal has remained extremely important in my work. When I work at pottery, I do it always with a feeling for quantity production. I turn it out rapidly instead of lingering over each piece. I decorate a dozen plates at one stretch, and as I pick up each plate I have no idea of what is going on it, except that it must be a free expression of something I believe in. I stack plates and tiles and bowls densely in tiers in the kiln, with little shelving; nothing to insure against warping or being scarred by the stilts.

All of this is, I recognize, perhaps a futile attempt to combat the sterile preciousness of the "artist potter"—a hateful term. Since there is no tradition, I wanted to create one of my own and work in it in community with the great traditions of the past.

In all the arts you may push the emphasis this way or that, develop one aspect at the expense of another, but to crow unduly over your little differences is only a mark of immaturity, and to live in a state of undue excitement over fancied newness is only a mark of boredom. If, as a potter, you are bored with symmetry and you find that in symmetry you cannot express your unconventional spirit, then of course you go in for "free form," and asymmetrical shapes. But the finality of a circle as concept and as actuality is rather hard to overcome, and pots, I imagine, will continue to be mostly round.

For I believe that the only essentially new thing in a work of art is the freshness of a new person and his fresh discovery of the world, of a spirit that expresses itself with confidence and freedom. There are periods in art which are to some extent revolutionary, when new forms seem to be evolved, but most of even this apparently startling newness is seen in retrospect to be a sometimes conscious rebirth or reaffirmation of old forms. When tradition and conservatism settle like a pall over a whole generation, then more violence is required to break out of it. But now, partly I believe because of the universality of reproductions of art of every kind and of every age, our live and *immediate* traditions have been replaced by endless influences. Extreme individualism, therefore, and the self-conscious search for originality are our curse. But each new birth is a recreation. In outward form and even inward spirit it is close to a repetition, but to command attention the new work of art should not have to express itself in new forms any more than a new baby has to have four arms in order to be an individual.

To maintain this subtle difference that is yourself is difficult, very difficult, and cannot be done through self-consciousness. To know yourself is the hardest knowledge to acquire, and it must be arrived at quietly and obliquely. You can never really see yourself, or smell yourself, or be fully aware of that emanation which is yourself. The more self-knowledge can be left to instinctual behavior the better. If you turn a spotlight on self, it vanishes or becomes a self-conscious actor. The truest approach to self-knowledge is to forget yourself in the problems of knowing and doing. To tell a student to express himself—to look inward—is the most futile of all helps.

Things evolved from self and self-absorption fall surprisingly into repetitive patterns, whether behavior patterns or speech patterns or patterns in painting. That's one of the most significant of Freudian discoveries—how alike people are. And these patterns, in whatever art, are the sure road to the academic unless they are enlarged and made vital by a passionate apprehension of the universe outside yourself.

Large goblet, by H. V. Poor

Bowl, by H. V. Poor

Harmony and order are in themselves easily achieved in the vacuum when form is divorced from content. The ability to make harmonious color and ordered form arrangements is an almost universal ability. But to give meaningful order to the universe by creating and arranging vital and living images—that is another thing. And it is only as the abstract qualities in art are welded into this total that they acquire any rich and emotional values. To accept these qualities as ends in themselves denotes such a paucity of faith, understanding, and, yes, just sheer energy as to be a saddening thing. It is settling for much too little.

The feelings, the concepts, that begin and end in yourself are only the starting points, and your creative richness is measured by the love and understanding with which you see and meet the world in its infinite variety and unexpectedness.

Romantic love is, I suppose, a practically universal concept. Young boys and girls can be desperately, passionately in love with love. They feel in themselves all the imagined attributes of love and feel rich in themselves because of their longing and the purity and strength of their passion. This is completely academic and according to pattern. Even the aberrations of love fall into secondary patterns. But *understanding* starts only when the loved *object* appears and is deeply, penetratingly perceived and loved for its own sake. Then vagueness is replaced by the exact sound of a voice, the specific and unique shape and movement of a body, the feels and smells and the whole emanations of another person, probably surprisingly different from your dreams. Through all these miracles that enrich your senses you enter into a creative life.

Renewal of contact with our world is the most necessary of all motivations to fresh creation. Our world has got too confused and complicated with too much knowledge of the wrong sort. We run around feverishly in automobiles; we ponder relativity, the fourth dimension; we are obsessed with instability and fear; we project ourselves into space. "Space" is the password in all the arts. "Space division" is the ponderous obsession of the painters. "Time, Space & Architecture," the title of the most popular *avant-garde* architectural treatise, is didactic and assertive, contributing nothing but new word combinations for old concepts.

A changing emphasis in relation to old concepts is, of course, part of the breath of life in new creation, but excitement over novelty is a poor substitute for understanding. If a young painter is excited about space he must see how Tintoretto and Rubens lived and moved in space, and how Giotto appreciated the elegance of flattened space, for nothing sound and fine can be built on denial.

Understanding is a formidable word, but for an artist it should be mostly of the heart and the eyes and the hands rather than of the head; yet it is important to have no mists of obscure words between yourself and your world.

In making clay do and be what you want, the hand is not only the master tool, but it is of itself your complete tool kit. Stone requires chisels and mallets at the very least to make it responsive. Wood, too, even the softest, must be whittled or chiseled or sawed into shape. Even paint, which in its simplest form of colored mud is, after clay, the most basic medium of expression, requires a brush or knife to control it properly. This rapport between the hand and clay has been the source of the particular and compelling appeal which pottery holds, but as mechanization and machine processes are more and more substituted for the hand, the product loses its human identity and, beyond purely use-value, we become indifferent to it.

To be a skillful potter requires above all skillful hands, and no dexterity with tools can substitute for that. You *feel* the texture and plasticity of a clay. You *feel* the strength and thickness of the walls of a pot between your thumb and forefinger. No instructions in "how to do it" can go far beyond the sensitivity of your fingertips and the intelligence of that most miraculous of all tools, your hand.

Pottery making, therefore, is probably the most primitive and the most sophisticated of the crafts—sophisticated because the hands of skilled potters have never been content to let a pot alone as soon as it merely functioned. When you become acquainted with the tools and utensils of primitive people, you will discover in these artifacts an astonishing universal instinct for style. Faced with an insecure life that

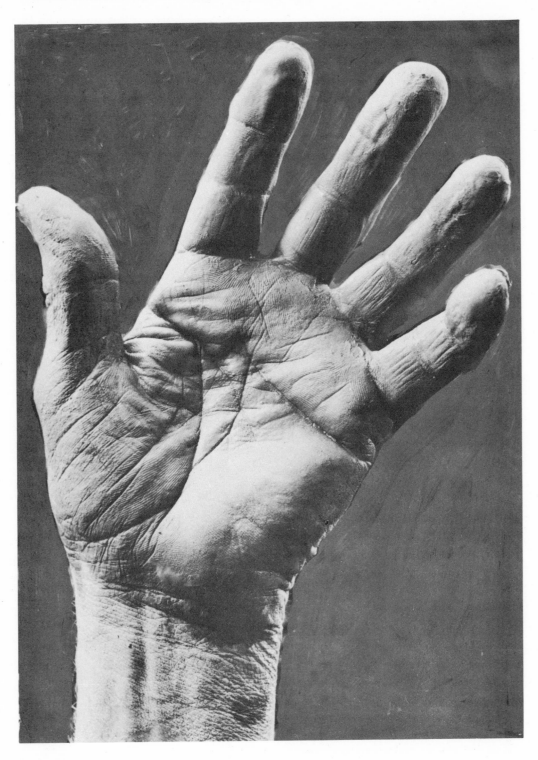

[47]

supposedly left only the slightest margin of time for leisure and the making of other than purely utilitarian things, primitive people still let style far outweigh functionalism in most of the things they made. Present day scholars give religious significance to many of these excursions away from the bare and practical attributes of their life. I have never felt that such an explanation was necessary or valid. Style arises out of love and understanding of a material and the creative artisan's instinct to see what he can make the material do. As he became skillful, and since he was not producing in quantity for a general market, early man pushed each thing he touched beyond the "good enough" into something that pleased and astonished him and his neighbors. This, I think, is the basis of style.

(right) Two delightful inventions obviously arrived at through putting together separately thrown pieces. Jugs from Cyprus, c. 2000 B.C. (Courtesy of THE METROPOLITAN MUSEUM OF ART)

[48]

(above) Perfection of style arrived at by a skillful potter, showing how delicately he could throw and how beautifully he could use the brush. From Iran, c. 4000 B.C. (Courtesy of THE METROPOLITAN MUSEUM OF ART)

[49]

Two pots from Costa Rica made much later than those illustrated on page 38 but in much the same cultural stage, showing how a kindred spirit achieved equal style on another continent. (Courtesy of THE AMERICAN MUSEUM OF NATURAL HISTORY)

Style in iron working. Mangbetu knives from Africa (Courtesy of THE AMERICAN MUSEUM OF NATURAL HISTORY)

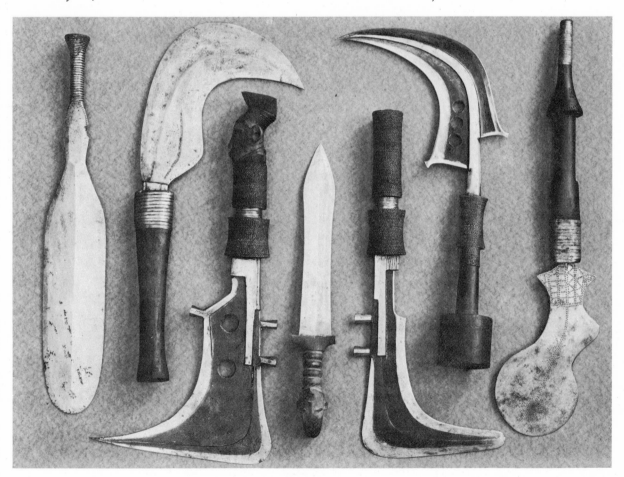

CHAPTER FOUR

Making Pots

AFTER THE HAND, there are tools of immense importance to the potter. I will list those I find most essential. For the simplest way of potting, hand building either through coils or pressing, nothing but skillful hands was needed; but the sticks and stones and bones that the first potter could find around him helped in scraping and shaping his forms. Refinements of those tools are all you need now. A metal scraper and a curved, flat bone for a template are good.

In neglecting the most simple process of building either pottery or sculpture with coils of clay, I do not mean to belittle it, but as I have never used it extensively myself, I am sure that anyone interested can get more help on procedures from other potters or books.

The early Mayan, Peruvian, and Mexican potters probably made all their pottery through coiling, pressing and building without use of the wheel, and their pottery and clay sculpture is as rich in invention, in subtle and noble forms, and in the refinements that come from skill and aptitude in handling their clay, as the pottery of any people of any other time. Being hand built, pottery becomes sculpture—and sculpture, pottery—with an intriguing ease and oneness of approach that is rich in inspiration for present day sculptors and potters. The variety and inventiveness of forms from this early pottery of the Americas can be matched only by the earliest Stone Age unglazed pottery of the Greeks and Persians and Chinese, all of whom obviously used the wheel with great skill and with such excitement and fresh inventiveness as to make later pottery from these same lands seem stilted, repetitive, and over-stylized.

Throwing

To turn his pot easily as he worked, an early potter set it on a flat stone; as he turned it, he got the idea for a potter's wheel, the one great and essential tool for anyone seriously wanting to do pottery. The idea and the mechanics are so simple that very smooth and beautifully running potters' wheels were almost universally in use wherever fine pottery was made. I am sure that within the lifetime of the very first man who made a potter's wheel, he had one running almost as well as today's, and was able to throw pots with great refinement and precision. The skills of an artist do not depend very much upon an accumulation of data or knowledge. Mostly they are born in him and die with him. The records of other artists are of immense importance in enriching his understanding and feeding his spirit, but the *doing* must remain so simple that the beginning and the end are within his grasp.

I will describe the potter's wheel I made when I started to do pottery. Now it may seem primitive to the point of affectation, but remember this was 1920; there were no "artist" potters' wheels and kilns on the market that I knew of and I had no money to buy them anyway. Maybe I have exceptionally strong atavistic instincts, too. I had never seen a potter throwing on a wheel, but I had seen those early unglazed Cretan cups and bowls at the Metropolitan Museum and knew that if

[53]

those primitive people could do such things so could I. And I had to find some way of earning a living through work that I loved to do.

In a junk yard I found an old washing machine flywheel, weighing twenty pounds and measuring about thirty inches in diameter, with a 1½-inch core for a shaft. In the woods, after much looking, I found a white oak stick about forty inches long and two inches in diameter with a sharp crook in it. I cut it and trimmed the end near the crook. So trimmed, it fit into the 1½-inch core of the flywheel.

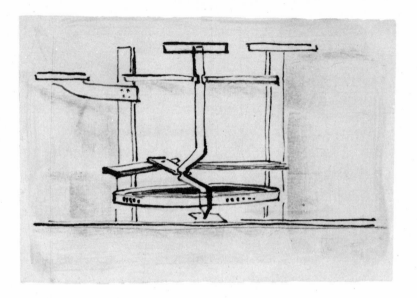

Then I set a long, round-headed screw into this tapered end of my shaft. I cut a deep, flat groove at the most offset point in the crook, about five inches over the flywheel, and another groove about five inches below the top of the stick. Then I made a solid frame of 2x4's, calculated to fit my shaft, with a dented steel plate for the sharpened screw to revolve on, flat leather straps for fittings around the oak shaft, and a top with two notched boards supporting the shaft at the groove five inches below the top.

When I had the shaft mounted, firmly held, and running smoothly, I cast a plaster head ten inches in diameter over the squared end of the shaft, and while the plaster was still soft, revolved it and trimmed it to run truly and accurately. On this wheel I learned to throw, and on it for ten years I earned my living. In 1930 a poet friend who had a machine shop replaced my wood shaft with a steel one, my leather bearings with roller bearings, and the plaster head with a steel one. Otherwise it is unchanged; and whenever I demonstrate throwing on other wheels, I find I like mine better.

Whether you make your own or buy one, or have a machine shop make it to your order, you should have a wheel. It is one of the delights of handling clay. When you have acquired some skill, you will find that the rapidity with which you shape and form, the sensitivity of the clay to every pressure of your fingers, the swelling or contracting or extending of the changing contours of your pot, make the whole process of throwing an endlessly inventive contest between your willful hands and the live but limited character of the clay. It is very like drawing. As a line in drawing can be alive and moving or, following the same contour, be dead and static, so the contour of a pot can live under your hand or become trite and common.

Throwing a Simple Bowl

On the metal head of your wheel attach a plaster disc of about ten inches in diameter and one inch thick. Stick it firmly with wet clay and see that it is exactly centered. To do this easily I have four shallow holes drilled in the top of the metal head and half a dozen bats which I cast and trimmed in place on the metal head. Uneven spacing of the holes makes the bats easily returnable to exactly the same place, and this provision is important in case you are working on two-piece throwing. One bat may remain on the head for months and be your regular working surface, but if you are doing two-piece throwing, or if you have a very fine but fragile thing which you cannot move safely from the wheel, the detachable bat is very handy.

Whatever you throw on the wheel must in the end be removed

from the wheel with as little jarring and deforming as possible. Potters who throw one form over and over, or who make heavy ware, can remove the finished pot by cutting it from the head with a wire and lifting in onto a slab. I have admired and tried to emulate this method, and very often could, but in general each thing I throw is an unpredictable experiment and by the time the clay and I have come to an agreement, the resultant pot is too fragile to stand such treatment. So I have on the shelf at my right hand a stack of stiff paper squares of varying sizes from four to ten inches, cut from black building paper. Using very wet clay, I stick one of these paper squares of appropriate size on the absorbent plaster head and trowel it firmly down with a spatula. On this I throw the ball of clay. When the piece is done, I raise a corner of the square, slip a wide spatula under it, and lift the piece onto a drying bat made of a flat asbestos shingle, halved. I find these paper squares better than thin plaster bats since, being non-absorbent, they hold the moisture in the base while the body of the piece becomes firm enough to handle for trimming—which, as I will explain later, has several advantages. Also, since they are flexible, I can peel them from the base easily if I do want the base to dry quickly.

I suggest a simple open bowl as the basic form to throw in learning. In its most primitive form it can be useful; in its most refined form it can be very elegant. If your work can be useful from the very beginning, the way to becoming a professional may open more quickly. And I hope that is the way you want.

Your clay should be very thoroughly wedged by being repeatedly cut over a wire and slammed together again on the wedging bat. It should be firm but not hard. Press a slab between your palms, stand it on edge and see if it can support its own weight. A basic principle of all clay work, pottery or sculpture, is that the clay should support its own weight. When the wire-cut surface is smooth and even, cut it a few more times for good measure, and then make a half dozen round balls about baseball size. Put these conveniently at your left hand, a bowl of water just in front of you and beyond the wheel, and your spatula and drying bats at your right, and you are ready to turn out pots.

Spin the wheel rapidly to the left, counterclockwise; press your wet thumb down onto the center of the plaster head, then aim and slam a ball of clay, flattening it onto the wet centered print of your thumb. If you miss by very much, pull it off and try over and over until you can hit close to center. Then, with the wheel spinning rapidly, plunge both hands into the water, press the palm of your left hand on the top of the spinning ball and the palm of your right against the side. Hold your arms very firm and rigid—make the clay do the shifting, not your arms—and in an almost instantaneous operation center the clay. Try this over

[57]

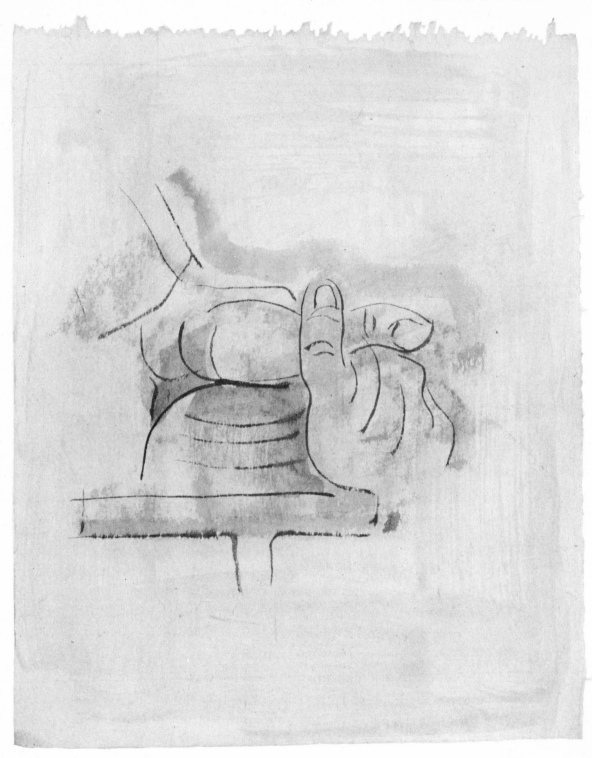

and over until you succeed fairly well and have a spinning shallow crater of clay which moves evenly against your rigid hand. Dip your hands in the water as often as necessary to keep the surface lubricated. If you try to be a perfectionist at this point, you will save yourself disappointment and trouble later on.

When you have reached the very considerable achievement of a centered crater of clay, relax and think of the next step. To make this into a thin-walled bowl, decide now how open or how tight you want

the bowl to be. How thin the walls are to be will decide itself, depending on the nature of the clay and your skill. Two things will determine the shape of the bowl—remember, clay must be *pressed* into shape by you, but the revolving wheel tends to *stretch* it through centrifugal force. As long as it is *pressed* it retains its strength. When it is *stretched* it soon gets flabby and collapses.

Remembering these things, set the wheel spinning again rapidly, and press your left thumb down into the center of the crater until you judge it to be a shy half-inch from the head. These judgments will soon become instinctive and suprisingly accurate. Now your two hands must work, the left inside, the right out, as forms between which you press the clay, making it rise as the walls are squeezed thinner and thinner. While the bowl is shallow you gain strength and rigidity for your hands by overlapping the thumbs.

If you want to carry the edges up straight, keep the finger *inside* firm and straight to serve as a template while you crook the ball of the outside finger, lifting and pressing inward as you raise and thin the wall. As the bowl spins, repeat this operation over and over, keeping the inside finger still but using an upward stroking movement with the right finger. As the wall rises to touch your thumbs, your hands must work separately, but the most heavy and resistant mass of clay has already been brought into an even-walled low bowl. At this point any lack of balance and symmetry in the walls (caused either by failure in exactly centering it, or by uneven hardness in the clay) has resulted in an uneven height of wall. If so, use a wire or needle to cut the uneven top down to an accurate level.

Stop and take stock of what you have.

Before you pull the walls higher, now is the time to establish the base of your pot—to feel the correspondence between the inner and the

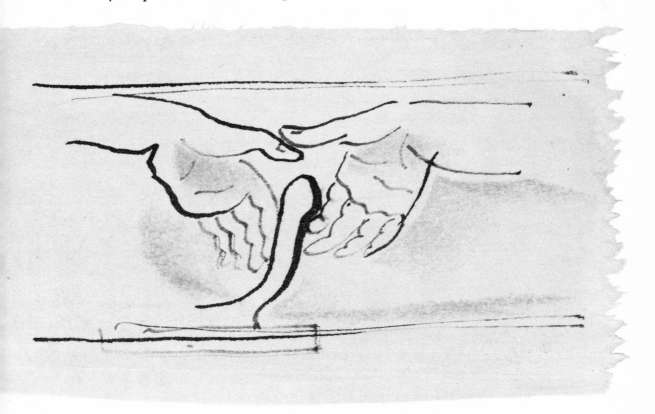

outer surfaces, and trim or push back into the walls any sprawling clay at the foot. You can press the walls at the base into almost their final thickness, which will depend upon their ability to carry the total weight of the wall. The total weight of the clay is the same whether it is still in a fat mass or pulled up into a tall wall. Also, if you want to pull the top of your pot in as it rises higher, this will be the last time you can get at the lower inside wall. You can test the thickness of the bottom by sticking a needle through to the hard base. You can calculate how much you want to spread, or retain, the walls. You judge the amount of spare clay you have around the foot and decide whether to work this up into the walls, to cut it away (the bowl of a spoon is an excellent tool for this), or to leave it to help reinforce the weakest point, which is the overhang at the foot.

Now spinning the wheel moderately, and with plenty of watery slip for lubrication, you can often finish the bowl with one steady, strong upsweep of your hands, keeping the fat top of the wall in the crook of your right finger, raising and pressing against the rigid left finger which you incline outward or inward, depending upon the shape you want. If you do this rapidly and with decision, the resulting walls will be free and alive with strong ridging both inside and out.

To have a fine surface for decorating, I generally use a template on the outside in finishing so that the finger ridges appear only on the inside. A smooth, flat, curved rib bone is my best template. If you

slightly thicken and round the top of the wall of your bowl with a soft sponge, you will give it strength. In heavy ware a strongly flattened top edge allows the lower walls to be quite thin with no loss of strength.

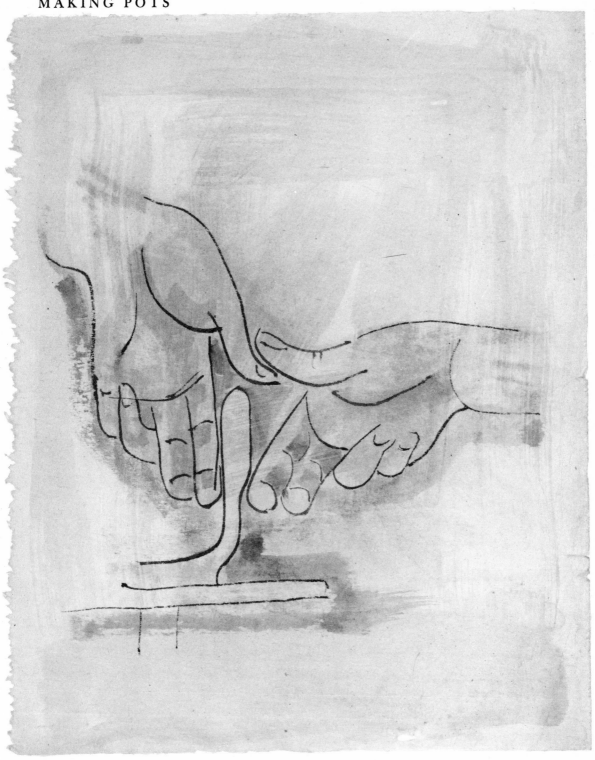

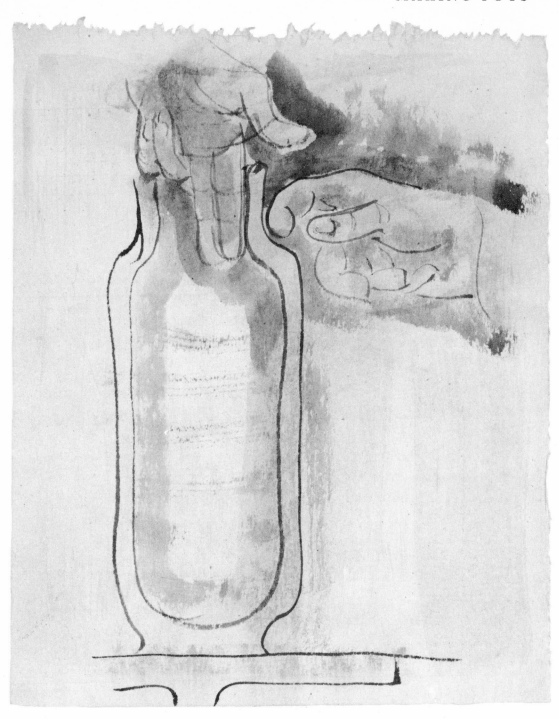

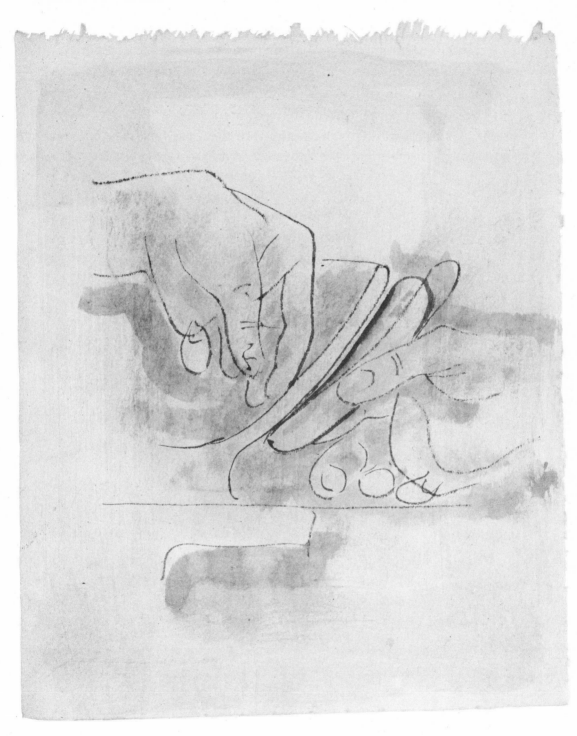

As you lean over the bowl working on it, you cannot judge its contour accurately. I have a mirror set to reflect the contour from the back, but in the last refinement of shaping I always slip off the seat, stand at arm's length with eyes on a level with the pot and give the final swell or flattening which makes a living contour.

This seems long in telling, but the finest forms are made rapidly

and in the course of doing what approximates quantity production. If I am going to make any bowls at all, I try to make at least a dozen at a time, and about three minutes to a bowl is average throwing time. But I often spend an hour at the beginning trying unsuccessfully to get the exact form I want on a single one, starting over again time after time.

Trimming

With your pots on the shelves drying, study the problems of trimming. As regards form, pots can be put into two categories: those that rise strongly from the base, and have a firm grip; and those that have a floating quality of elegance, being borne on delicate feet. Many in the first category do not need trimming; the vigorous plastic form that is given in fine skillful throwing, with economy of clay from top to bottom, is enough. But those rustic pots, with such excess weight at the bottom that they shock your hand when you try to lift them, are sad specimens. As you make pottery and handle it, you become conscious of cross sections through the clay. Your hands feel beautiful form inwardly as much as your eyes see it outwardly.

Assume that the bowls you have thrown are like this drawing. When you are fairly skillful, they come from the wheel much like this—

the lower sides and bottom only a little heavier than the upper walls. They really need no trimming for ordinary table and kitchen use. They are light, strong, and pleasant to handle. While they are still moist in the bottom you may press the bottom center up a little to be sure they have bearing along the outer edge, not the center of the base. But your early efforts are more apt to look like this, so a little refining will help.

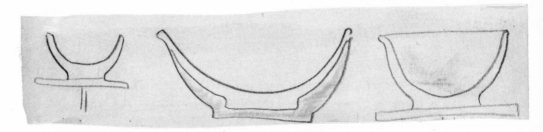

Your pot is tough now and leather-dry. Feel the bottom and the walls and estimate how much you should cut away. Scrape the plaster working head of your wheel clean. Put the pot upside down as true to center as you can. A series of different sized circles scratched in the plaster will help. Spin the wheel at moderate speed, holding a steady right finger against the foot of the bowl, and tap with the left hand to shift the bowl slightly until it turns smoothly against your stationary finger. Considerable practice is necessary to accomplish this quickly. When it is centered, press it firmly down with the left hand while you stick it securely with soft clay all around its edge. If it has a wide top and does not require much trimming, four spots of clay will hold it.

For all operations on a plaster head, the plaster should be moist. When it gets soaked, the clay will not stick, so replace it with another. When it is dry, the clay dries too quickly and separates from it.

[68]

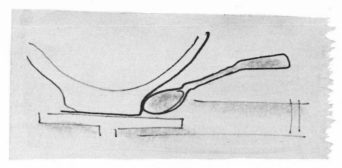

Now you are ready for an operation exactly like turning wood on a lathe. The tools you need you can make easily to suit yourself, or buy. One of my most useful tools is an old teaspoon. When you take excess clay from the foot of your pot after you have finished throwing, the rounded point of the spoon reaches in under the overhang, cuts the clay cleanly away and leaves a pleasantly curved foot. With its edge kept sharp the spoon serves the same purpose in trimming, and the hollow of its bowl gathers the clay shavings neatly.

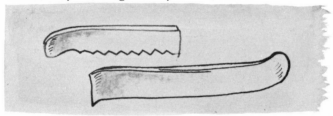

I accumulate tools; then use only one or two. These two are my mainstays, both drawn to half size. One is made from an old keyhole saw; the other from a flat steel band. Both the sharp-edged flat areas and the ends are useful for truing walls.

As the wheel spins, the clay comes cleanly off in long shavings if it is at just the right stage of dryness, and the whole operation of trimming is neat and exact and accomplished quickly. You may easily provide a rest for your hand, adjustable to any height by means of a notched stick on the shelf back of your wheel and a 1x2 resting on it. I have one, but I never use it, for I find that resting my left arm on the arm rest, with my left hand grasping the right wrist, gives enough steadiness.

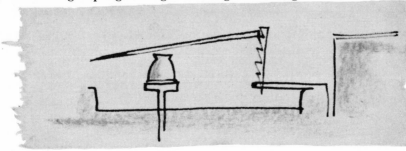

In all these operations of trimming and decorating that are done on the wheel, I control the wheel with my right foot resting on the fly-wheel—spinning, braking, and giving an exact, instantaneous control that is impossible by any other method.

The foot of a pot is as important as any other part of it and can make or mar the whole. I have always taken pleasure in a foot which reveals the inside contour and emphasizes the continuous shell of the pot, but with the same inside contour many different feet are possible. All of those suggested in the drawings are possible and equally good, but they completely alter the character of the bowl.

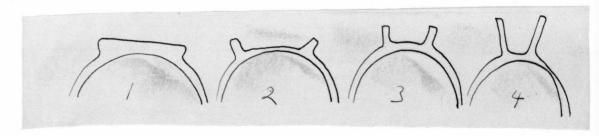

As I take each pot off its paper base, while its bottom is still moist, I test, by pressing, the thickness of the bottom and generally indent the whole center a little if it is quite thin. Then I know that I must work away from the center, leaving it only slightly touched.

As you trim, a quickly acquired instinct tells you when to stop. This comes from your sympathetic judgment of the whole curve of the walls of the pot. In the many pieces I have trimmed I have cut through very, very few.

The No. 4 foot you will recognize is not possible, starting from No. 1, without extending the clay in some way. When I want tall feet on a set of bowls or pots, I dry them rather rapidly, so the walls are tough while the bottoms, because of their paper bases, are quite soft. Then I combine trimming and throwing on the foot. By trimming I make this heavy foot. Then with a finger or fingernail on each side and with plenty of lubrication, I draw it up to this. A small template in each hand may help you to be firm with the stiff clay.

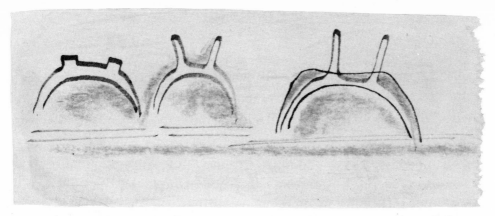

Both the throwing and trimming of more complicated forms comes with time and practice, but involves nothing new until you want to make two-piece pots. With skill and a good clay you can achieve large forms, even jug and bottle-like shapes in one piece, but they cannot be so light or delicate or so well controlled as those you can do with a two- or even three-piece throwing.

Two-Piece Pots

In the pottery of all countries where the wheel is used, it has been common practice to make complicated and difficult forms by joining together separately thrown parts. These parts may be spouts or necks or bases which obviously are attached after the main body is thrown. They may also be sections smoothly joined to add height through the main body of the vase or pot or jug. These, when skillfully done, are impossible to detect and the pot is fully as strong as though thrown in one piece. The ease of joining and thoroughly welding partially dried clay sections adds greatly to the free and inventive possibilities of potting.

I shall describe the procedure in making wine jugs or bottles, with a variety of shapes easily derived from the same procedure:

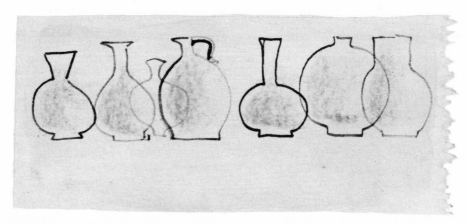

Throw a simple bowl with a rather wide base and firm, even walls. Set a pair of calipers to the exact width of the top, then set the bowl on its demountable plaster bat aside to dry in an even heat to avoid warping. Throw another bowl using a slightly larger ball of clay, bringing the top to the exact width of the calipers but leaving much more clay at the base and pressing through the clay at the bottom to the paper square. Put this to dry in the same heat, but wrap a wet strip of cloth around the base. While these are drying you might as well throw half a dozen matched pairs of bowls, so that you will not get impatient while waiting and will be able to make at least three or four jugs when you have everything ready.

When the first two bowls are leather-hard, put the second one on the wheel and trim the top to a slightly rounded edge. See that the bowl is true and round, set the calipers to its dimension, and set it aside. Put the first bowl exactly in place on the wheel. Check it with the calipers (you can expand it slightly to enlarge it or cut some off to contract it until it corresponds exactly to the other.) Trim its edge with a concavity matching the round of the No. 2 bowl, but press it into a slightly wider edge in order to have some excess clay for sealing and welding the joint.

Paint the edges of both bowls heavily with a cream-like slip made from the same clay, then set the No. 2 bowl upside down on No. 1, guiding the edges exactly into place, pressing and tapping down on the top bowl while you spin the wheel and press inward at the joint with your thumbnail. Peel the paper base off the top (formerly the bottom) of the top bowl and you can reach in with a curved stick to smooth and weld the

joint. Now you can draw the moist excess clay at the top (formerly the bottom of your No. 2 bowl) into a tall neck or spout or any form you wish. A joint well made and with the two sections at the same stage of drying is astonishingly secure. Seldom have I had one open either in drying or firing.

I have ignored the problem of a foot for your jug. Obviously the easiest is to have a solidly based foot that requires no trimming. You *can* reverse the first bowl, trim it and return it to exact center for the joining, but that obviously adds another difficult step. If the final top to your jug is too small, or perhaps has an irregular spout that prevents firmly up-ending it for trimming, you can throw a high-walled support of stiff clay which you keep on another detachable head to be used for trimming such forms.

In starting, you must have a clear idea of the final form of your jug so that the walls of both bowls pick up the desired direction at the point of junction.

Control and accuracy must be within your reach before you can do successful two-piece potting. In a hill town near Orvieto in Italy,

I watched the thrower in a three-man factory that turned out big red unglazed water jugs of the same shape used there since time immemorial. With the same exceedingly strong and plastic red clay that the Etruscans had used, and working on a heavy kick wheel, probably unchanged from the time of the Etruscans, he would throw a dozen of the large base forms, pulling them up to correspond exactly to the height of a stick he had; then a dozen of the small cylinders for the neck, working again until the edge of his cylinder came exactly to a stick he had set in clay beside his wheel. All was done with an astonishing ease and precision and speed, and each of the resulting big jugs had a life of its own, a conviction as to its right to exist almost but not quite to the pattern of the thousands that had gone before. This kind of authority, of unself-conscious use-beauty fusion, is as rare as hens' teeth in contemporary pottery.

Handles

As in so many things about pottery there is no clear definition of good and bad in all the various types of handles. If a handle for a pitcher or a cup or a jug is adequate in size and strength, which means it relates well in proportion to what it is on, and if it has decision and grace, it is then good. Where and how it is placed can be determined only in each individual case.

There are, however, two main classifications which can be made: formal and informal; and the two pages of illustrations show this distinction.

Informal Handles

In an informal handle the first necessity is that the clay be manipulated with skill and decision, so that the final result has the same sort of life that the well-thrown pitcher has. It should seem to grow from and belong to the pot, as the tail of a fox or a cat or a squirrel is distinct from but yet part of the animal.

With a plastic clay which has a minimum shrinkage, these handles can be attached and formed directly on the pot as soon as it is firm enough to be handled and hold the weight of the handle. The pot or pitcher or cup can be leather-hard and its foot already trimmed, but your handles can be slightly more wet and plastic—firm but still able to be bent and pushed into form to fit the pot.

In attaching such handles I proceed as follows: Assume you have thrown and trimmed a dozen cups similar in size and shape. Set them aside at your left hand. With the same clay, slightly stiffer than for throwing, roll a small tapered cylinder, about lead pencil size, between

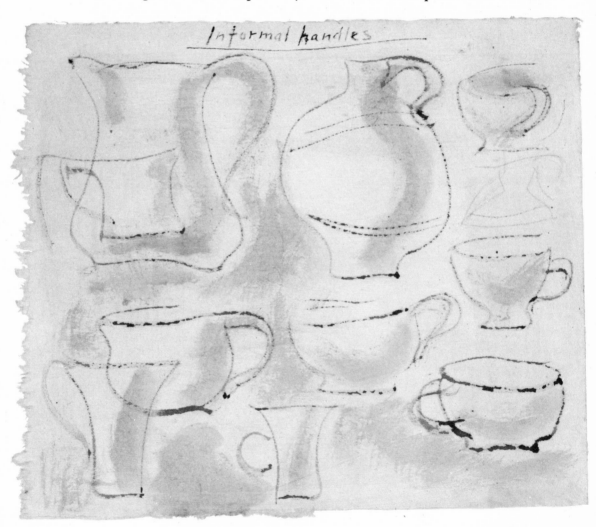

Informal handles

the palm of your hand and a moist plaster bat. Flatten it slightly, bend it, hold it against a cup, and try it for size and length. Make a dozen, maybe one or two extras, put them side by side on the bat, and with a moist finger flatten them as much as you wish. Then with your left thumbnail as a template flatten and enlarge the head of each.

Now take each cup on the palm of your hand, examine its profile to decide exactly where you want the handle to be, and with a brush stipple a large blob of thick cream slip onto the spots at top and bottom where the handle will attach. Now moisten all the top surfaces of your handles. The plaster bat will have dried the lower surfaces somewhat, making them stiff enough to hold their shape. As you pick up each cup you will find that the clay has become moistened around each blob of slip and the slip has become overly stiff; so scrape it off, add a fresh blob, and press the flattened head of the handle firmly into place, welding it securely and curving it to the curve of the cup. Bend the handle over your finger, wetting and stroking the top side if it is inclined to crack, and weld the flattened end to the lower spot. Now with the first handle, you can study the cup and make some decisions which may hold for all the other cups.

The decisions will probably be between these slight variations— all easily done and probably equally good. A round tapered stick like the handle of your brush is excellent for rolling down the protruding

slip and making a smooth job of the welding. If the handle sags, set the cup upside down as you finish.

This same procedure holds for pitchers or jugs. Its great merit is its plastic unity with the container and the freedom in variations to fit each thing most beautifully.

Instead of rolling each handle separately you can roll out a thin slab of clay, cut it into long strips of the width you want your handles, separate the strips, soften the edges, blunt one end and slightly taper the other, making half a dozen or more at once.

For large strong handles on big pitchers I thicken the edges of my handle-slabs. This gives them more life and strength than a flat slab has.

Do not attach a very wet handle to an overly dry pot or it will crack in drying.

I am fond of an informal *twisted* or *braided* handle and find that such a handle resists bumps and outlasts more dish washing than any other, because of the elasticity in the twist and the wide bracing of the braided handle. They must be done with decision and style. As the clay must be very plastic in forming them, it is best to make them, curve

them roughly to fit, and lay them aside to stiffen before attaching them, but they must not be so stiff that they cannot be modified and fitted to each form. Otherwise they become overly florid and frozen in character. Again remember that a sense of ease and plasticity is a great point in their rightness and style.

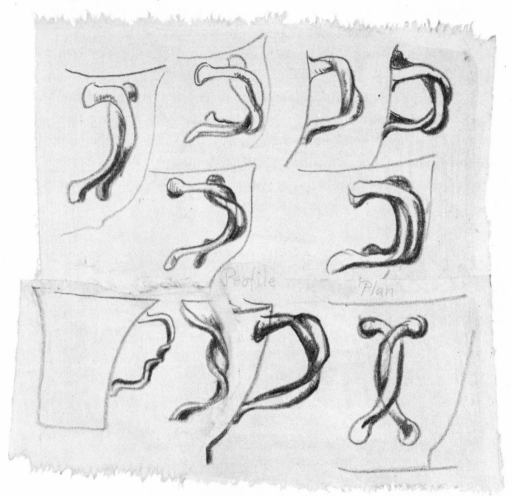

Formal Handles

Whether they are made by hand or through quantity production, certain types of handles are set and formal in character. If well designed, this is nothing against them. The thing to avoid is the appearance of being

[80]

stuck on, though in fact and procedure they are. But if they attach firmly and at the right place and are in right proportion, they can be right for whatever they are on. Such handles should be made after careful study and also probably after several drawings, or after different sized slabs and rolls are held in place for determining proportion, shape and placing.

Form the handle and set it to dry. When it is at the same stage of dryness as the pot (this should not be, for best practice, beyond leather-hard), hold it in place and carefully trim the ends to fit accurately the curve of the pot. Then stipple both ends and the points of junction on the pot with heavy slip and press firmly into place, using the slip which is pressed out to smooth and weld the joint. If both pot and handle are still soft enough for some pressing and shaping with a small round stick the result can escape all sense of rigidity.

For clarity I have separated the working of handles into two methods, formal and informal. In practice, however, you will use a combination of both methods.

formal handles

Plates

Plates can, of course, be thrown on the wheel, but since they exist primarily for only one surface and therefore as thrown forms are very limited, I have made them in the simplest way over plaster forms. Thus I can complete the foot speedily in the same operation as the plate.

I have a dozen or so plaster forms of varying sizes and different profiles which I pour and trim to shape in shallow circular dams of clay which I make on my wheelhead. While the plaster is still soft but set enough to build into a mound, work rapidly to trim and change this form to any sharp or flowing profiles that you want and that represent in reverse, of course, the hollow of your plate. You may trim and modify it later if the plates you make on it do not please you.

When the plaster has set, detach it from the wheelhead and make many other moulds. To detach it easily, set several wooden wedges around the edge, partly under the clay wall of your retaining dam, and paint the wheelhead with a thin jelly of soap dissolved in water. Let the bats not only set, but let them dry out completely before you use them. Otherwise the clay will not separate cleanly from the plaster. Never return clay which has been used with plaster to your clay bin, as small particles of plaster will expand in firing to ruin whatever they may be in.

When the dried bat is ready for use, center it on your wheel—which is done automatically as the center spur of your bat slips into the depression in the center of your wheelhead—then moisten it slightly. Do not soak it.

On a square of heavy duck about 12x12 inches beat and roll out with a heavy rolling pin a large pancake of clay, quite stiff. Make this pancake as round as you can, rolling from the center to the edges and leaving the center thicker, by perhaps $1/4$ inch, than the edges, which should be $3/16$ of an inch thick. Slide your hand under the duck and put the cake face down on a bat centered on your wheel. The clay clings to the duck well enough to make this easy to accomplish. Then pull the duck away. As you turn the wheel, trim the irregular edge of your pancake with a sharp soft wood wedge. Use a sponge and your finger, or a curved template, to shape the clay slightly, working from the center out to fit it firmly to your pattern, and to remove any air bubbles.

Scratch a circular line where you want the foot of the plate to be, and on this line press a coil of clay made from the trimmings of your plate. Shape this coil into as flat or tall a foot as you want. I generally make a foot with an outward flare so a wire can be tightened around it for hanging as a plaque. You can, of course, extend your foot into tall stands for compotes, and also make elaborate edgings on your plates.

Before taking the bat off for drying, slightly press and thicken the edge of the plate and with the soft wedge see that the clay is not welded to the bat. If your clay is stiff, you will find that when it contracts it will pull itself off a fairly steep-sided bat—how steep you must find out for yourself.

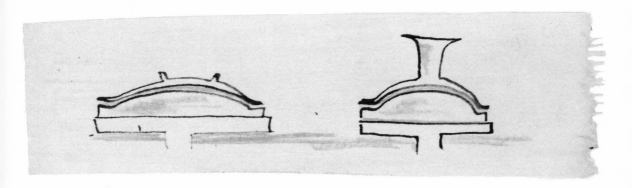

Tiles

The simplest, quickest way to make tiles is to roll them out on coarse burlap with a heavy rolling pin. To insure even thickness you can roll the clay out between two flat sticks of any desired thickness as guides.

Lay a stiff paper pattern of your tile on the clay slab and cut away the excess clay with a sharp narrow wooden point. Lay your drying bat on the tile, flop it over and remove the burlap. When it is fresh and upside down, I often groove the back with a wire cutting tool to make it lighter and reduce warping.

Flat tiles are more apt to warp in drying and crack in firing than plates or bowls or any forms which have some convolutions to take up shrinkage and give strength through a change of direction, just as corrugated sheet iron is much stronger and stiffer than a flat sheet. So dry them slowly on flat bats or pieces of asbestos-concrete shingles, or pieces of any kind of wallboard. Turn them if they warp, and when dry enough stack them flat, four or five high. But when they have once dried, always stack and rank them edgewise, since any weight on a slightly warped tile will break it.

Plaster of Paris

Gypsum—plaster of Paris—has many uses in a pottery because of its characteristics in relation to clay. Quickly setting, strong but porous, its absorbent quality dries and shrinks damp clay enough to break any bond between the two. Consequently, for moulds in casting, or as bats on which to work, it is almost indispensable. Get it at any lumber yard as Gauging Plaster in fifty pound bags.

Since wide variations in its density (that is, the proportion of plaster to water) are fairly unimportant and will vary greatly with the use to which you put the plaster, I will give only the simplest way to handle it; the variations you will be able to work out yourself.

In an enamel basin put a quart of cold water. Into this, using a coarse sieve for dipping, sift plaster until it rises in a mound through the water. Then with your hand stir the mix, seeing that the plaster blends evenly with the water. Stir and wait until the mixture begins to thicken; then pour it into moulds, or onto flat glass for small bats, or begin to trowel it on for plastering or building up surfaces.

You can make your plaster very dense and strong with larger proportions of plaster, or more open and absorbent with less. Powdered alum in the water slows the setting of the mixture and allows you to use it over a longer period. If possible, clean all tools and vessels before the plaster sets, but do not send the residue down any sink drains, as it will quickly clog the pipes.

A plentiful supply of large round bats is good to have. You can make them most easily on a wheelhead, which should be about fourteen inches in diameter. Around its edge wrap and tie securely a two-inch strip of leather—a piece of old machine belting, for example. Slather the wheelhead with clay slip or a jelly of soap and pour this form full of plaster. In a very little while you can jar it loose, remove it, and repeat the process until you have all the bats you need.

Plaster bowls are good for drying out clay. Make them by pouring plaster over an enamel wash basin turned upside down and surrounded by a leather or clay wall for a dam. In both the plaster bats and the plaster basin you may bury strips of canvas or coarse string soaked in plaster to serve as reinforcement.

CHAPTER FIVE

Decoration

SOME ABSTRACT PAINTERS like to call a painting an object, with the wish, I suppose, to have it seen and appreciated in the same detached way in which we see and appreciate an object, but I don't think any strictly two-dimensional surface can be an object in itself. In a limited way a sheet of paper or a flat canvas is an object, but when its prime function is to carry lines and colors and be hung on a wall, then its *object* quality, never very strong, completely vanishes and it becomes a medium of communication—a picture of some sort, vapid or eloquent, living in a world of its own, its boundaries fixed by a frame. If it says nothing, it becomes non-existent; but it cannot escape from *saying* into *being*. When the Museum of Non-Objective Art in New York hung a Cézanne portrait unframed on a bare wall the attempt was to make it an object, but since it was obviously never made to be considered as such and had no identification with the wall, this attempt became an abortive gesture.

Mural paintings that retain the quality of walls, and tapestries that are in themselves beautiful textiles, are objects, with the subtle

Plate with sgraffito design, by H. V. Poor

union and conflict between the object and imagery which is so elusive, so easily overbalanced in one direction or another, but which in balance has such a powerful appeal as to make the distinction between Fine and Applied Arts entirely non-existent. Decorative painting is essentially boring, I suppose, because it decorates nothing. It does not have the vitality gained from meeting the demands of a containing object. An *area* can be decorated, but *space* cannot be decorated.

Since the beginning of man, objects made from clay have invited surface enrichment. On pots, plates, urns, tiles and all manner of other ceramic things, men have put many of their richest and most fresh and inventive images and have arrived at simplifications and symbols which have enriched all the arts. The techniques used in this decoration are endless and varied. They all partake of the miracle of fire, of the transformation from swift fluid movement, which registers every certainty and every hesitation, into the permanent and eternal certainty accomplished through the white glow of heat.

Drawing with a brush, scratching, pressing, modelling, and overlaying are the most common and easiest ways of decorating. Variations of these are endless: from the dry, unglazed and earth-colored pots of the American Indians, to fatly glazed and brilliantly colored Persian pots. Variations in style are even more endless: from the geometric design to the realistic modelling of Palissy ware. I think you will be lucky if you don't know too much, but do have some overmastering loves and enthusiasms to give you steadiness, and some consistent direction to keep you from the great engulfing amalgam of present-day technical competence and conformity and forced self-conscious attempts at originality.

I started doing pottery for the pleasure of decorating it, of having something entirely in my control from beginning to end, so that both the object and the images it held would be equally mine. Loving drawing and painting, I followed wholeheartedly the technique which I felt demanded least technical and scientific knowledge and gave most freedom and richness to drawing and color. From the beginning I had an obsession against letting technique be the controlling factor. I even

Wine jug, 8″ high. Sgraffito decoration in copper red. By H. V. Poor

Vase, 6″ high. Pale blue slip brokenly flowed over dark purple ground. Sgraffito, with a dark aura of iron sulphate around the fish. By H. V. Poor

exhibited and sold cracked and imperfect pieces if I felt the decoration was fine enough, as you would mount a drawing, if you liked it, even though the paper was torn and soiled. As time went on, my increasing skill and my instinct for craftsmanship made me more exacting; but my sole criterion is still the life of each piece, and its beauty of form and decoration, not its technical perfection.

Methods: WHITE SLIP, SGRAFFITO, BRUSH DRAWING

If you carefully cut into the petal of any brilliantly colored flower, you will find that the brilliance is obtained through a very thin film of color over a pulpy and opaque white center. To obtain a brilliant and transparent color in ceramics you must work in a similar way on a white ground.

If any white-burning clay and the high temperature required to mature it are in any sense close and native to you, then this is the clay you should use; but the high temperatures will very much reduce the color range you can get. The simplest thing to do is to use a white slip over the red or buff or tan body of whatever native low-firing clay you have.

The Haverstraw clay which I dug and used through all the first years of my pottery making is a very fat blue clay which at 05 to 08 fires a fine red color. It takes and holds a white slip beautifully and has a fine fat character under a raw lead glaze. When I corrected its excessive shrinkage and fatness and short firing range by adding sand or grog or more refractory clays that I got from clay banks near Woodbridge, New Jersey, it served perfectly as the body for the decorated plates and tiles which I wanted to make and for low-firing pots and bowls.

The slips you use will give you different effects according to the way you apply them. I generally *pour* my slip over bone-dry ware

Goblet, 6" high. Broken white ground. Sgraffito line drawing with pale yellow on the fruit. Decoration surrounded with the blue stain of cobalt sulphate. By H. V. Poor

[91]

Bowl, 7″ high. Sgraffito through a heavy white slip. Glaze carries a faint stain of copper sulphate which, in the reducing fire, develops irregular red-purple areas. Pale blue stain around the leaves and birds. By H. V. Poor

using a flat ladle to dip and pour. Often I use a very thin slip, planning upon its being partly eaten off by the glaze to give an irregular broken effect. Let the slip flow rapidly over the dry surface. If your clay is a sandy porous clay, many tiny air bubbles cling to it and give a speckling of dark through the slip that is very pleasant.

Tiles I *dip* rapidly with a rolling motion in slip poured into flat trays, getting a solidly opaque or a brokenly transparent surface, depending upon how rapidly or slowly I move them through the slip. In this operation, as in practically all the operations involved in decorating and glazing, it is the exact and skillful manipulation, the dexterity of hand combined with experience and imagination to guide you, that is of much greater importance than formulas are. The same slip, the same glaze, can be used either for uniformity or for varied and imaginative results.

Bowls and plates I first half fill with slip; then pour it out with a rotating motion which completely coats the inner surface. Flattish bowls and plates I often leave without slip on the outer or bottom side. Hold a pot by its foot in your left hand and turn it while you pour slip over it with the ladle in your right hand.

Strong and heavy ware can be slipped, decorated, and glazed while still raw, and can be finished in a single firing. To give more quality to the white slip, and more sharpness to the etched line in sgraffito work, I often apply a black slip to the raw ware, fire it once, then apply a white slip, decorate, glaze, and finish it in a second firing. This makes handling easier, eliminates unsound pieces, and gives a hard smooth surface against which sgraffito lines move more evenly and freely.

Sgraffito work is done best while the slip is still damp; so is free brush drawing and the laying in of color areas. If your piece becomes too dry, moisten it by quickly dipping it into water or spraying it with water. Either way, however, has a tendency to blister the slip. It is better to plan your decoration well in advance, and work quickly while the slip is still moist.

On pieces too complicated for dipping or pouring, you can apply the slip with a wide, soft, long-haired brush. Also, undoubtedly, you can apply it by spraying, but I have an aversion to all spraying techniques—carried over possibly from my dislike of air brush effects in painting and the universal use of spraying, to such deadly uniformity, in all commercial ceramics.

What to Put on Your Pot, Plate, or Bowl

To decorate beautifully you should above all draw beautifully; but beautiful drawing lies in decision and clarity, in expressiveness rather

than accuracy, in sensitive judgment of scale and placing in relation to the object, in those qualities perhaps included more exactly in the word "design," with both its French and Anglicized meanings; that is, drawing with all parts well related to each other and to the containing space.

In both sgraffito and brush drawing a sure but rapid movement over the surface is important. Lines in themselves can be fumbling, static, and dead; or sharp, moving, and alive.

One of the most effective enrichments of a surface is simple cross hatching. Try this in both methods, brush and sgraffito, moving very swiftly but within defined rectangles.

Try endless geometric patterns and combinations. These have been and remain wonderfully effective when finely related to the shape of the bowl and with effective variations of filled and empty spaces and of different colors.

In all fine ceramic design, abstraction and imagery are combined. The images may become geometrical symbols, but their imagery is essential and basic. The lines above and below the band of images, the judgment as to how thick or thin they should be, how many of them, where placed in relation to the lip—all these are judgments in purely

Plate, 5″ in diameter. Heavy white slip carrying some manganese sand, over a purplish brown under slip. The darks are supplied by the slip being cut away. By H. V. Poor

abstract relationships. They are never in conflict with imagery, representation, or symbolism, but are in perfect accord. It is the balance and restraint one puts upon the other that makes a complete work of art.

Obviously, a purely representational image thrown haphazardly on the surface of a jug is boring. To my great surprise I have found that highly elaborated abstract decoration on the surface of a jug also becomes dry and boring. Personal imagery stays perennially fresh and engaging, and when you come across it in contemporary decoration, it seems like a breath of life.

Living Lines

First, the brush itself is immensely important in obtaining a living line. On the absorbent ground of your moist pot you must use a brush that will carry a great deal of pigment if you want a long free line. Since you want also a line that can go from thin to wide, you must have a brush with very long bristles that point perfectly.

At a good art store examine the striping brushes and the long-haired lettering brushes; also the long sable brushes made for ceramic decorating and set in quills, which you can mount on a round handle. Japanese brushes are not bad but are too short-haired. The long sable brushes are fine for striping but are too limp to respond accurately to the abrupt changes in direction which make for lively drawing. Get all the brushes that appeal to you and try them.

For sensitive and free but controlled lines, you can make brushes very easily. Get a discarded, much worn, very long-bristled house painter's brush and cut tufts of bristles from it varying in thickness from lead pencil size down to $\frac{1}{16}$-inch size. Try to keep them as they were in the big brush, for the bristles lie close together and their ends have worn fine through use. Holding each tuft firmly, squeeze Duco cement over $\frac{1}{2}$ inch of their base, work it through the bristles, and wrap the

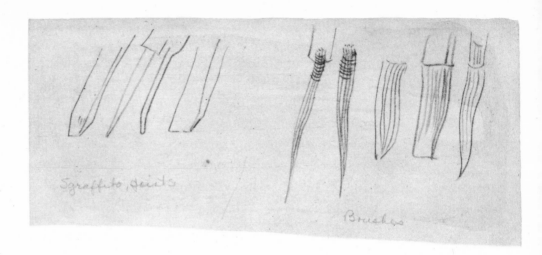

bundle firmly with strong thread. You can get a beautifully pointed but firm and well-controlled brush with bristles as long as 2½ inches; this will be ideal for all brush drawing. Use a metal ferrule for mounting on a handle, or drill a hole of required size in a dowel, or make a ferrule of Scotch Tape, securely binding the bristles.

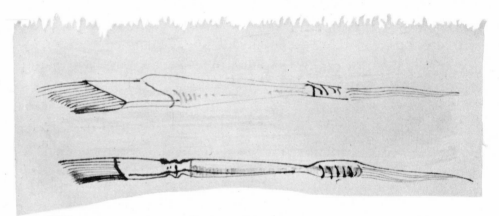

Pigments and Mediums

Your pigments are, of course, oxides of all the metals. You will gain a great deal in the beginning if you leave prepared underglaze colors alone and get acquainted with the metals and the colors they give you under different heats and different fluxes. As you buy them, they are mostly black (a few are dull brown and yellow) and they develop their color only when fused into the glaze. Copper, manganese, iron, and cobalt are the most common and the most useful. The exciting colors that come from these black oxides are part of the endless enchantment of the fire. These oxides are finely ground when you buy them. I mix them with water plus a little binder—gum arabic, or gum tragacanth, or even molasses—and keep them in clearly labelled little screw-topped bottles.

For a good black take two parts black iron oxide, two parts manganese dioxide, one part black oxide of cobalt and grind them together on a sheet of glass with a palette knife, adding only enough water and some binder to make a heavy paste. Grind this mixture until all grittiness has gone. Transfer the paste to a small flat plate that you can hold easily.

Dip your long-bristled brush into some free water lying in the rim of the plate and thin the edges of the paste enough to give a fluid but heavily pigment-charged load to your brush. Roll the brush on the plate to point it, and stroke it until it does not drip. Now make a free steady line, rich in pigment. The long bristles will feed the line over a surprising distance. On an eight-inch plate turning on your wheel, one charging of your brush gives you a complete rich line at the rim; that is, a line twenty-four inches long. Make your mixture thick or thin, until it does what you want it to do, and is properly adapted to the porosity and the consequent pull of the surface you are working on. The same technique is used in brush drawing on paper, enabling you to get rich blacks or the palest grays.

For laying in colored areas, flat brushes are better.

Sgraffito is probably my favorite technique. It gives me complete freedom but more sharpness and more exact control than brush drawing, and in firing it stands all heats and even gains in emphasis as the colors almost burn out or the glaze runs. The etched, indestructible line gives a pleasant definition to the often floating quality of color. With sgraffito, I often use for color areas the water-soluble metal salts, such as copper and cobalt sulphate, which penetrate and stain the whole slip, never obscuring the line and giving an integration with the body of the pot more than applied pigment can.

[99]

Vase, 6" high. Sgraffito drawing. Some dull reds from copper, with a smoke-gray glaze blistered from excessive reducing in an open flame. By H. V. Poor

Design for portrait plate by H. V. Poor

In making a sgraffito line, you commit yourself with a positiveness which demands the greatest surety, and this entire elimination of tentativeness is its charm. The Pennsylvania Dutch Sgraffito plates were decorated by very unskilled draftsmen who had to make positive statements. Images of charming clarity and simplicity were the result.

I do all my decorating at my wheel, where I can use striping and free drawing as I want, and where the wheel used as a turntable allows me to study the roundness of my surfaces, the adjustment of my objects, and their scale to the total spaces. If you want, you can draw on your slip with colored inks; they burn out in the fire, and you can then draw in sgraffito after you have rightly placed or drawn whatever you plan. I always do whatever planning is necessary in small drawings on paper, so that on the freshly slipped pot or bowl or plate I can have the pleasure of making every line, every adjustment of my image to the shape that contains it through the quick, instinctive judgments which I trust more than I do my considered ones. If they are slightly off, their freedom makes up for their lack of perfection—a non-existent quality anyway.

For tools use nails, dentists' tools, wood points, or wedges, so that you can get thin or wide flat lines from the same tool.

Colored Slips

I often use colored slips laid over each other in areas closely related to the decoration and plan. On a white slip I loosely draw with a colored slip, drawing in masses rather than lines; then I use a strong sgraffito line or a sharp brush line for more exact definition. It is an endless technique that invites new experiments. Don't let them lead you down the path of empty tricks, however, and remember that all techniques are a means to an end, not the end itself.

I have talked of decoration fitting the form, and perhaps some

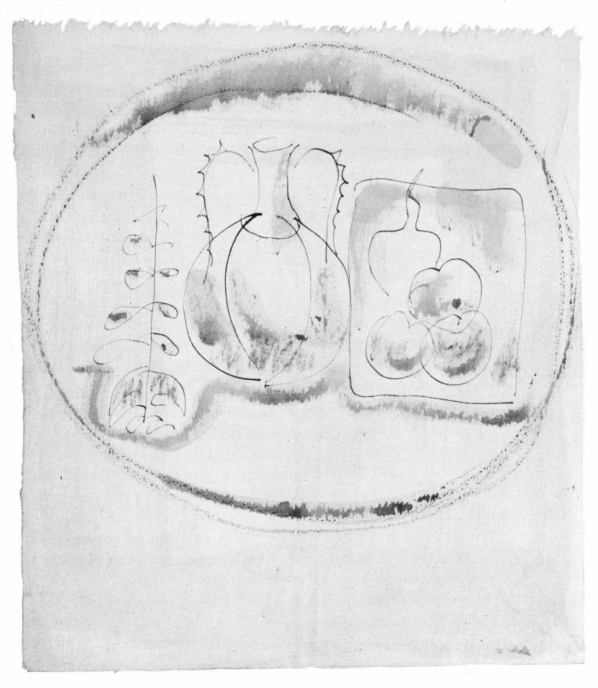

Design for plate by H. V. Poor

attempt at defining this very indefinite phrase may be helpful. But it must still be vague, for good design is not subject to, nor does it arise from, rules. It is unpredictable until it is done; then it seems inevitable.

Decoration may also be divided into two obvious but helpful classifications: formal and informal. As you study a thrown form, its unity may be extremely single, or you may be quite conscious of the diversity of parts that contribute to the whole. Decoration can enhance either aspect. A pot springing from a tall or slender base and then swelling outward into an open body invites your eye to a consciousness of its stem as opposed to its fullness. Horizontal banding, with lines or tone separations at crucial structural points, emphasizes this difference; and different horizontal banding is the traditional and universal starting point of formal decoration.

The first question I always ask myself as I pick up a jug or a bowl or a plate to decorate is, do I want to band it and so confine the decoration to areas, or do I want a completely free decoration? If I am exceptionally pleased with the form, I generally decide on free decoration, and often the exact placing of a single unit of decoration, contrasting with the untouched unity of the whole, has a remarkable unifying effect, or seems to enhance the form. It should certainly never detract from it. Nor should the divisions of beautifully judged formal decoration ever hurt the form. It is true, however, that an imperfect or mediocre form may be made exciting and rich through fine and original decoration, and certain weaknesses of, say, the foot or belly or shoulder of your piece may vanish under beautiful surface spacing. To accomplish this, a certain shock value to your eye is important, such as tone divisions at unexpected places, or decorative asymmetrical and very positive forms. Picasso is adept at hiding the dull, weak forms on which most of his pottery decorations are put.

Even with the less differentiated shape of plates, the same problem is basic. If you are particularly pleased with the way the flattish bottom rises and flows over the rim, you would put on it a free decoration or one that is confined to the center, rather than an insistent all-over pattern.

Sketches for plate decorations by H. V. Poor

CHAPTER SIX

Studies in
Design

IN ADAPTING realistic natural forms to the more formal images required in pottery decoration, I have always tried to express the third dimension in two-dimensional terms. The Greek vase draftsmen did this, but in general all the primitive decoration which we so much admire today accepts the most two-dimensional aspect of the forms used. The attempt to formalize the third dimension leads to a much more varied and informal pattern than the strictly two-dimensional patterns.

The Italians and the French have, of course, done some very lively and beautiful, fully modelled and realistic painting on ceramic ware. If this has style and grace, we accept it for what it is and are glad for its existence; but it has nothing for us today, as it contributes nothing truly belonging to ceramics. It belongs much more to painting, and, in fact, is mostly overglaze painting fired at very low temperatures.

Although made in the Bronze Age, these three forms from Cyprus are clearly evolved from a skillful and inventive use of the potters' wheel. In decoration they show a delight in brush work, in the opposition of straight and waving lines, in the sparkle of shapes and tones which come in cross-hatching, and in simple geometric schemes based on open and closed squares arranged in checkerboard pattern. The round-bellied jug has an extraordinarily fresh and non-symmetrical breaking up of space with grouped lines and banding placed in the most effective way to emphasize the full round belly of the jug. (Courtesy of THE METROPOLITAN MUSEUM OF ART)

The first and most powerful controlling factor in simplicity of design lies in the technique itself. If you decorate on an unfired, absorbent surface where you cannot change or correct, then submit this to the accidents of a covering glaze, and trust it finally to the mercy of the flames at white heat, you will not be tempted to go in for detail. The simplifications which result from this technique are the tools which you should use with imagination, taste, and a fresh inventive eye to arrive at your own personal imagery and patterns.

If you have a live surface to start with—the swelling, curving walls of a well-thrown pot—and an envelope of glaze with its own transparent or translucent or richly opaque quality, you have an extraordinarily tactile reality of surface. So in breaking up this surface with decoration, whatever you do by shifting the quality of colors and patterns will only be the *suggested*, the *indicated*, the *pretended* illusions of reality, which is the realm of art.

For myself I like to set up tensions and conflicts between flatness and depth. I like to surround my sharply designed images with the cloud of a stain of color so that the images slightly float on the surface. I like, even on the same piece, to contrast flat and deep, and formal and informal, decoration. The object itself welds all these differences into a total unity, if they all have the sympathy and the character given by the same controlling hand.

Surface textures can play an important part in unifying the design by preserving an insistent surface quality. But contemporary painting as well as much contemporary pottery is leaning too heavily on this factor, to the detriment of clear and convincing design. The beauty, and the appeal to the imagination, of fragmentary, half-destroyed antique works of art, as revealed through photographic enlargement and exaggerations, has played a large part in this cult of the lost and found, and of the obscure. Insofar as it has re-emphasized the material and put it in contrast with what emerges from the material, it is good. It can and often does sink into shallow artiness, however, and thus becomes a refuge for incompetence.

Although the use of the potter's wheel seems to have been unknown in Peru, the fine fat roundness of these jars is a demonstration not only of the skill of the clay workers, but of the basic economy in strength and material of a sphere. In decoration they represent a perfect fitting of simple striping, banding and stippling to the form, with the most keen awareness of lively variations between masses and lines and of oppositions introduced into rhythms to avoid monotony. (Courtesy of THE AMERICAN MUSEUM OF NATURAL HISTORY)

*These two Cypriote vases from the late Bronze Age are clearly inven-
tions arrived at through putting separately thrown pieces together with
great pleasure in the contrast and abruptness of the different parts. The
full handle bridges the differences and plays an essential part in the
unity of the off-balance total. The gracefully careless brush work on
one, and the single spiral welt on the other are perfectly in keeping with
the light spirit of both forms. The tilt probably happened in the drying,
or it could have happened in the firing; at any rate, it did not worry the
potter or it would have been corrected.* (Courtesy of THE METROPOLITAN
MUSEUM OF ART)

The full round sphere of this white painted Cypriote vase of the early Iron Age, from which the delicately modulated neck rises, is one of the hardest forms to achieve in throwing. The decoration of circles arrived at through varied and ingenious placing of the finished form on the wheel makes this whole vase an expression of a skillful potter's delight in his wheel. (Courtesy of THE METROPOLITAN MUSEUM OF ART)

A wheel-thrown Cypriote vase of the Iron Age. The delicate, shell-like quality of the form poised on its stem, the accuracy and delicacy of its banding and striping, the effective grouping of lines against open spaces, and the way a single decorative motive is tellingly placed in each open space, mark this as a work of an extremely sophisticated people. In the interior banding, see how the placing of the one wide dark band, well down from the edge, gives great delicacy to the lip of the vase. (Courtesy of THE METROPOLITAN MUSEUM OF ART*)*

A tall bowl. An extremely simple undifferentiated form, with the belly flowing softly into the abnormally large foot. A slight pulling-in at the top tends to give a very contained monolithic quality to the form. Decoration is sgraffito with a formalized still-life placed informally; no containing boundaries except the outer forms of the pot itself.

[113]

A formal pitcher with both spout and handle abruptly set into the body. Decoration is free sgraffito fruit drawings set off informally. The single objects are rather large in scale for the pitcher. The important thing is that the lines should be sensuous but abrupt, echoing the shape of the pitcher.

[114]

A tall goblet with a tall, delicate foot. Pulling in the walls just before the flare at the top gives a floating character to the form. Two formal bands of white slip with brush decorations on the tan body informally cut across the white bands.

A bowl with a low foot tucked well in under the even curve of the walls. No emphasis whatever at the lip, one of the most cozy and compact forms possible. One band runs low under the curve, but broken wave-like bands occur irregularly through the design as a symbol of water.

For lightness' sake I like a story-telling design. Far from subtracting, it adds one more quality to the complex that makes up enjoyment. The story-telling and humor involved must be purely visual.

I like jugs with the top and bottom almost equal in height and girth with a slightly elongated globe in between. There is a balance here between a monumental built form, and a light soaring form, which gives it a very complete and self-contained character.

The story told on this jug records a minor tragedy in my own household.

The flow of line enveloping this form from the curving lip through the softened foot would be hurt by any break of banding.

The informally placed design grows from the foot and expands in about the same ratio as the body of the bowl. Drawings of birds from the Florida Everglades supply rich material, with a style which would be hard to equal.

[119]

A wine jug which starts abruptly from the ground, with no foot, and ends with an upward reaching neck. The white slip ends irregularly short of the base. One band emphasizes the slender point of the neck. The sgraffito decoration is of grapes and foliage.

(top) A bowl with a white slip on dark ground and sgraffito decoration, rather overly full. It has taken me many years to realize how effective empty spaces can be. (bottom) This straight-sided bowl with pouring spout makes an effective use of open space, and exploits the thick and thin possibilities of a free sgraffito line.

[121]

CHAPTER SEVEN

꙰

Ceramic Sculpture

THE GREAT HIGHLIGHTS of sculpture, the great masterpieces, probably have not been made from clay; but the record of man as we know it in clay-built images is, I think, the most warm, most personal, most endearing of all the records he has left.

In the art of making images with clay, it is vitally important to emphasize *making* or *building* as opposed to modelling. It is this characteristic of being *built* with clay that most clearly distinguishes ceramic sculpture from sculpture in any other medium. It is from this purist point of view, that of a *structure* in clay, that I think I can be most helpful. By sticking to this approach you will be likely to arrive at freedom of expression and at fine simplifications derived from your material—which are of the essence of all imagery—more quickly than through any other method.

[122]

Bullock-drawn cart and two grooms. T'ang (Courtesy of MUSEUM OF FINE ARTS, BOSTON)

The clay most adapted to building is a shorter clay than is best for throwing. Add sand and grog to your regular clay until it does what you want it to do; that is, to hold strongly to whatever shape you put it into, to shrink as little as possible and still be plastic enough not to crack or crumble when you bend rolls or sheets of it into form.

The tools you need are a rolling pin and a variety of cutting and modelling tools, which you can buy or make. Wild cherry is a very common bush or tree and has a firm, pleasant wood from which to whittle variously shaped tools, which often can follow the sensuous curves of the branches.

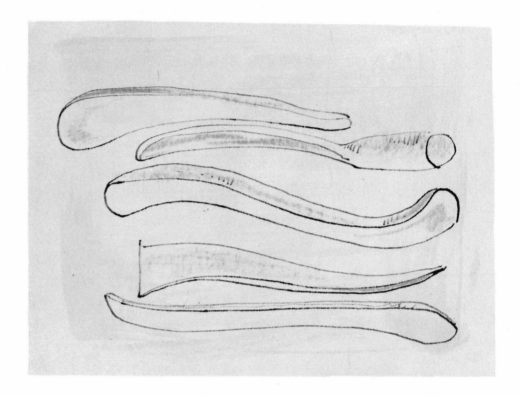

If you whittle them out, scrape them to a velvet finish with broken glass, and oil them; you will enjoy using them more than the ones you buy. Metal scrapers and wire cutting tools, however, you may as well buy. Old hacksaw blades are useful tools. A few pieces of firm duck or any strong cloth on which to roll out your clay, some slabs of board or plaster, and a sheet of light, flexible cardboard complete your essential equipment.

The basic thing for you to remember is that the pieces of clay from which you make your structure must all be of approximately the same stage of dryness so that their shrinkage will be the same. A wet piece stuck to a much drier piece pulls itself off in shrinking, even if you have done a good job of fitting and attaching it with slip. But in a short clay with little shrinkage, quite a range between wet and dry is feasible, provided that even the hardest pieces still hold a lot of moisture. Most of the shrinkage occurs as the clay loses its plasticity.

[124]

Building

I will pass over coil building here, as I did in pottery making, because it is so simple that it offers its own solutions to whoever is doing it, and also because it entirely lacks the stimulating, exciting suggestions and simplifications which come out of building with the more structural units of slabs of all shapes and sizes. Building with slabs is carpentry, masonry, pattern-making, and sculpture all in one.

The Chinese potters loved to make little temples and houses and miniature terraced gardens of clay. I would advise you to get familiar with your problems by studying and imitating them. In the Museum of Fine Arts, Boston, for example, is a bullock cart which is a beautiful thing and structurally within your ability. The principle that a clay structure must be planned to support its own weight does not mean that it cannot have some assists, provided these do not violate the unity of the whole; but try to get along without them as much as possible. The bullock cart obviously could have been set on a low box or on another lump of clay while the wheels were attached.

To begin, roll out on your pieces of duck several slabs of clay with variations in thickness from ¼ to a shy ½ inch. Put them aside to stiffen while you plan your work.

When your clay slabs are firm but can still be bent without cracking, plan a little house, or whatever appeals to you. Reduce it to patterns, the outlines of which you can scratch on your clay slabs. Then cut them out with any slender wood or metal point. In all cutting of clay it is not the sharpness of the edge but the slenderness of the tool that is important, since it is the clay clinging to the sides of even the sharpest blade which offers resistance to cutting. This is why a wire or a needle set in a wooden handle, or a hacksaw blade ground to a long needle point, are the best tools for cutting clay.

You can bend and scrape and fit the units of your structure until

they please you. Then roughen the edge of your clay pattern with the hacksaw blade, paint it heavily with a creamlike slip of the same clay, and put it in place, pushing it down firmly and squeezing out all the slip you can. This is generally all you need to do, but if you want to make the joint doubly strong, or want to smooth it to hide the joining, you can lay a tiny roll of soft clay along the joint and smooth it in with a blunt-nosed tool. Lightly tapping the piece along its other edge with a flat wooden tool effectively welds it. Whether your forms are simple or complex, this pattern way of building invites invention and is astonishingly strong and sturdy in the firing.

Heads

I shall describe a simple and effective way of setting up a head in terra cotta, which you can use as a basis for much careful and realistic modelling, even portraiture, or leave at any stage you please between being pottery or sculpture.

From a large slab of ½-inch thick clay cut a rectangle about 8½ by 11 inches. The head you are starting to make will be slightly under life size, and this slab is to serve as the neck. Bevel both of the shorter ends. This slab is to be rolled into a cylinder and stood on end.

Once on end and the two bevelled edges welded, this piece will be quite strong and will support itself; but until then it is rather tricky to handle. So roll the sheet of cardboard, which I listed as part of your equipment, into a tube about two or three inches in diameter. Lay this on the clay with one end of the cardboard cylinder flush with a long side of your clay rectangle. On this paper cylinder you can roll the clay slab, letting the cardboard unroll just the necessary amount to serve as a core for your clay. On this support you can overlap and weld the tapered edges with slip. Then with the whole upended on a board slab, contract the cardboard cylinder by twisting its inner edge until it leaves the clay standing free.

Reach in with your long curved stick to smooth and weld the joint firmly. Expand the bottom slightly for a firmer base, weld it to the board with clay, and put it aside to stiffen and become strong enough to support the head.

Now make the head itself, again using a ½-inch thick slab to roll a larger cylinder. Support it by means of your cardboard, and upend it on another clay slab which will serve as a base. Do not make the walls of this cylinder more than about six inches high; that is, reaching no farther than the top of the forehead. If taller, they become too flabby and difficult to handle.

On the clay base, shape this second cylinder somewhat to the shape of a head, with a pointed oval for chin, and a more full round for the back of the skull. Weld this form securely to the clay base, which will serve as the underside of the chin. Trim the base flush with the side walls of the cylinder.

While these two essential parts of your structure—the head **and** the neck—are drying so as to become more set and firm for further work, plan the structural characteristics of the head you want to make. Whether or not you want it to be a portrait, you should start with a very clear idea of the type of head you want.

Even in making a portrait head, I never work from the model. I study my subject carefully by making about four drawings from front, side and back, studying particularly the facial angle—that is, primarily, whether the forehead overhangs or is set back of the lower face, or continues in the same direction. Note, too, the comparative width of the head at the temples, upper forehead, cheek bones and jaw bones. If these big characteristics are true, you will find resemblances convincing from the very start. If they are not right, any work on the details of features will be wasted.

Your work on the head now *with the top open*, will give you tactical knowledge of the vast difference between *making* and *modelling*. With one hand inside pressing outward against the hollowed palm of your outside hand you establish the structural swellings of brow and

[128]

cheek bones, nose and mouth. With the outside hand pressing the clay into the bowl of the inside palm you make the big depressions of eye sockets, temples (if they are hollow), and the depression under the ears between the jaw and neck. Wherever the clay is pressed to the point of cracking add little slabs inside or outside for reinforcing.

This hollow clay shell, with its simplified structural swellings and depressions, is often astonishingly expressive. Expressiveness in clay is what you want, and it is often gained at the expense of literal accuracy. In making a thing of clay you follow the demands of the clay. Modelling, by contrast, is apt to be too representational, too literal, too much a copy.

In pushing form out from within you arrive naturally at a sense of swelling and expanding which is one of the finest attributes of sculpture and hard to achieve through any cutting away process.

In the big hollows of the eye sockets draw the eyes with a pointed tool, and build the upper and lower lids with strips of clay rolled or cut accurately to form. Draw the mouth, and add clay for the lips if you want them full. Attach shell-like clay slabs for the ears, studying their placement very carefully.

Up to this point your clay head is a bowl-like form as much like a pot as like a head. To carry it further, you should put it on its neck so that you can study its set and its tilt and make decisions about what you want to do with the base and the top of the head and how far you want to carry the detail. If your clay is good, and if you have been working rapidly, with your clay shell no drier than necessary to be firm, you can add little slabs and rolls without the use of slip as a binder.

When both the cylinder for the neck and the bowl of the head are firm enough to handle freely, you can trim and shape the two parts to fit well at the angle you want. Then set the head in its place on the neck cylinder, using slip to make a firm union. It is well to cut away the base slab of the head where it fits over the hollow of the neck, so that you can work inside clear down to the wooden slab at the base of the neck. Thus you can make a smooth, strong joining, and push neck and head into a continuous form.

For shaping clay after it is too stiff to push or pinch into form, light taps with a paddle-like tool can do a great deal of changing—indenting or swelling or warping the form with considerable freedom. Up to the point of almost complete dryness, this tapping is effective to make slight modifications.

The head on its long cylinder is not very stable. If you want just a head, cut the neck off with a needle wherever you want, and weld it to a clay slab of whatever shape you want for a permanent base. If you want a more elaborate structure, you can decide now what you want either by making drawings, by cutting some paper patterns, or by holding various slabs of clay in place to get suggestions. This is one of the beauties of all work in clay—you can solve things as you go along, when inventions come as much from the material as from you.

It is very much in the tradition—Chinese, Etruscan, Greek, etc.—that the base be a dome-like form. This carries the head high, gives it a firm base, and suggests the shoulders even in its most simplified pottery-like form; or it can carry great elaborations that go with the character of the head above it, as do Donatello's powerful portrait busts in terra cotta. So I suggest that you construct a sort of basic form which you can leave simple if it pleases you, or elaborate infinitely. At any rate, it will firmly support the head as you work further on it, and allow you to tilt it forward or back or sidewise without getting it off balance.

From a ½-inch thick slab cut a collar-shaped piece (see drawing),

and from it make a simple cone shape and fit it around the neck, welding it firmly, and placing it high or low on the neck according to whether you want a long or short neck. This can be done with the single slab, or with two or even several slabs. Then onto this cone weld two epaulet-shaped slabs to widen the dome and suggest shoulders. When these pieces are firmly joined and well placed, let them rest and go back to finishing the head.

With the method of working clear, and with a solid firm head set up, procedures from now on must be your own. You can add, subtract, and model on this basic form as much as you want. You can keep it moist so that you can work on it indefinitely. You can keep it very simple, and define the features merely by drawing on an almost blank egg-like head.

You can build up as elaborate a structure as you like to top off the head. I build onto the bowl-like form gradually, keeping a hand hole in the top until the very end and cutting inner walls away where strong outer walls have been substituted.

If you want to build out heavy swellings for the hair, do so with thin slabs just as you made the shoulders. You can texture the hair with a toothed modelling tool, or by adding little free strands of clay. Possibilities are endless, and the enjoyment you get out of the clay structure is translated into the total enjoyment that your finished work gives.

When you are ready, you can easily seal the top with a well-fitted slab and weld it on with slip, smoothing and flattening the edges as thoroughly as you wish. By using a small tool with a flattened end no bigger than a lead pencil, you can smooth and break edges down bit by bit without exerting pressure enough to disturb the main shell of your form.

Before the base of your head dries enough to start shrinking, loosen the whole sculpture from the wood slab with a thin spatula or a wire to prevent its cracking. To have a firm edge which will resist chipping before and after firing, run a rounded tool or a rounded wire cutter around the base where it meets the slab to get something like this.

Maine Truckdriver (slightly under life size). Unglazed, sandy, red-buff burning clay darkened irregularly in the flame.

Portrait bust (life size). Red buff clay, irregularly colored by fire.

Young Girl (life size). Dark, coarse gray clay. Unglazed.

Covered jar, 15″ high. Modelled doves on lid; sgraffito doves on jar. Dull red-purple of copper under excessively reduced fire.

Head, 6″ high. Pale buff clay with redder burning clay in hair. Stained in smoky flame.

(above) Clay head with wash of slip from Vera Cruz. (Courtesy of THE AMERICAN MUSEUM OF NATURAL HISTORY)

(left) Caricature of Ben Shahn. Buff clay keeping the texture of the rough duck on which the clay slab used in making it was rolled out. This head shows how practically all its modelling was done by pushing out or pressing in the original clay slab.

[139]

More Elaborate Sculpture

For a more elaborate structure in clay I will describe the making of the terra cotta stage-set for *Ten Nights in a Bar Room.*

On a square stiff piece of light wallboard lay a fourteen-inch square of duck, and on this roll a roughly round ½-inch slab of clay. Over it lay a fourteen-inch round plaster bat, slip your hand under the wallboard, flip the whole thing over, pull the duck away from the clay and center the plaster bat on your wheel. Trim the clay slab to a perfect disc, and on its outer edge erect a clay wall 2½ inches high. You can cut long 2½-inch strips of clay and weld them in place, truing them as the wheel spins. Across the center put two clay braces to help carry the weight. This is the base on which you will build the whole structure, so put it aside to harden slightly.

You should have a very clear idea of what you plan to do. I have quite complete visual images before I start making any plans or drawings, although they are always greatly modified as I work. The most

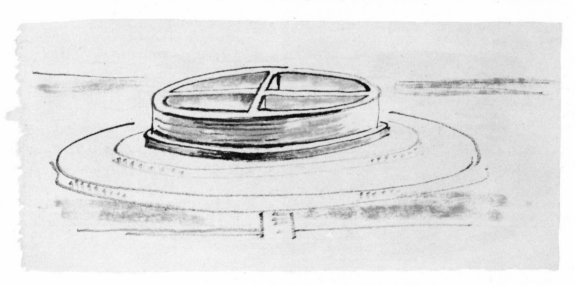

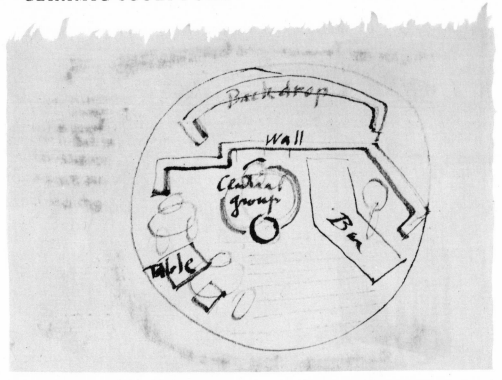

necessary thing is a clear geometric or structural plan for your sculpture; have the ground plan even more resolved than your concept of what the elevations will be. A sound, varied, three-dimensionally balanced geometry will produce a basic rightness much more important and much more constructive for the sculptor than any conventional regard for design in terms of catching light and shade in an interesting way.

On a circular piece of paper, the size of your base, draw the ground plan and indicate the placing of each element in your structure. Your problem now is to make all the parts to the same scale and to keep them and the base in the same stage of dryness so that in assembling them and joining them with slip, they will hold firmly together in drying and in firing.

To manage this, you need a damp-box—that is, a container where your clay will dry enough to be firm, and will thereafter hold an even moist condition. For a single piece of sculpture, such as a head, you can keep the clay in good working condition with damp cloths and a bag of air-tight plastic over the whole; but for parts of a more elaborate clay

[141]

*"Ten Nights in a Bar-Room," by H. V. Poor. Miniature stage set, 16"
wide.*

structure (and often in working with two-piece throwing) you need a damp-box to hold forms in a permanently moist state. I find galvanized iron garbage cans with firm lids very satisfactory. I keep them for storing clay ready for use and generally I have one or two only partially filled; so on this damp clay I press a flat board to carry my clay pieces, where, tightly lidded, they stay moist indefinitely.

The pieces in this assembly of *Ten Nights in a Bar Room* are made in the order of their structural importance, the big forms containing the smaller forms. The different walls of the room are cut as slabs from the same flat of clay and joined to each other and to the base at the same time, the frequent changes of direction giving strength to the whole structure. The flat slab along the top serves not only as a terminal trim for decorative completion, but for giving strength and rigidity to the flat walls. The back drop is curved for greater rigidity, each side being terminated by a cross-angled slab; while the top is crowned by a florid and typically clay-like terminal, to give contrast, lightness and humor to the whole affair.

The bar, the table and the two stools are the simplest of slab constructions. All these, when welded firmly into place, are quite strong and self-supporting. The stage is now set for the actors, and is put back into the damp-box while the little puppets are made.

Figures as small as these are made from solid rolls of clay, joined together with slip. For safety's sake, however, all the heavier parts, such as the torsos, have their centers gouged out with a wire-snare cutting tool. Then the figures are assembled, tried on the "set" for size and position, modified, fixed into place, and firmly welded to the floor and to whatever else they may be touching.

The whole is now ready to dry—very slowly, so that any strains and tensions set up by slightly uneven dryness of the parts can equalize themselves. It is best to keep the whole piece in the damp-box overnight before starting it to dry in a mild temperature—never in direct sunlight.

A structure like this obviously needs the lightness and the extra story-telling qualities which can be found in decoration, in the charm and variation of color and glaze. In this case, I used flat, pictorial decoration to extend the limited sculptural quality. In preparation for my accustomed technique of a slip with color and glaze added, I brushed a black burning slip over the whole thing as soon as it was dry and put it in a first firing, from which it came in perfect condition.

In considering how to decorate and glaze this, I felt that an all-enveloping fat glaze with no attempts at surface and texture variations would be most fitting and would most unify the varied parts of it. For color I wanted the simplicity of effect that lies in a very limited and formal use of color. The soft purple of manganese dioxide and the pale yellow of antimony make, together, one of my favorite color combinations; and these two colors, with a few red-browns in small areas were the only colors used on the piece.

Over the fired black slip I brushed a fairly uniform white slip, leaving it intentionally thinner over certain edges and areas where I wanted the dark underslip to burn through—the front of the bar, for example. Then through this slip I drew, in sgraffito, windows for the houses, pictures on the walls, a bar-room nude, features on the peanut-heads of my people and even a few clouds in the sky. To these I added a little color—purple and yellow. Over the coats of the men and the head-dress of the woman, I brushed manganese dioxide; and over all the arms, legs, faces, panels of the wall, etc., I brushed antimony oxide.

No attempt at a realistic flesh color was made. I felt that such concessions to realism would shift the emphasis into the trivial and sentimental. Although the subject in itself is trivial and sentimental, I wanted the treatment to dignify it, to symbolize the era and the point of view associated with the old play, rather than be actually of it.

In present day sculpture, as in present day painting, textures and textural variations are made much of. On the whole, I think this is meretricious, much overdone, and a sign of emptiness. The textures which result naturally from the materials you use and from your way of using them should be enough. Rough and smooth, fat and dry, are, of course, obvious surface variations within your reach in using and in glazing clay; but the unconscious fresh textures that come from skill and a direct purposeful use of the clay are most important.

If you are ambitious to accomplish large figures in clay, your ambition and your ingenuity must show you the way; and the accumulation of experience which you have put behind you must be very considerable if you hope to avoid disaster. Most clay workers gaze in awe and wonder at the over-life-size Etruscan warrior in the Metropolitan Museum, accomplished through building, undoubtedly; and one tries to figure out the many props and aids that those ingenious men must have used. With a very short and groggy clay you can have thicknesses up to two inches or two and one-half inches in safety, but avoid more. Most large sculpture and reliefs in present day use, done in terra cotta, are pressed into moulds made from a modelled original, and often fired in sections which are put together in the installation.

But since I am a potter, I will leave these large and complicated problems to the sculptors and be content with things that are within my own strength to handle, and that fit into my modest kilns. In this, no sense of sacrifice is implied either in present creative pleasure or in enjoyment of the past. The toy-like houses and the charming little tanagras of the Greeks; the masterpieces of the Chinese in clay; the pottery animals of the Peruvians and Mexicans and many primitive races—the world is rich in clay images as fresh and living and personal as the day they came from the fire.

For a terra cotta structure as complicated as the fountain I made for actress Helen Hayes, you must plan and work from a scale model unless you have the facilities to handle and fire the whole piece as one unit. But even if you did have a kiln big enough to take the whole thing—some six feet in height—it would be foolhardy and invite disaster for you to build, handle, glaze and fire the whole at once.

This fountain was to be set, slightly recessed, into a high brick wall running along one side of a garden.

In preparation for this fountain I made and fired four small but complete sketches about eight inches high and five inches wide—all differing variations of the same theme of "Leda and the Swan."

When we settled upon the sketch to be carried out full scale—the

"Leda and the Swan," fountain made by H. V. Poor for Helen Hayes. Figure of Leda 36" high.

figure of Leda is about thirty-six inches high—all the parts were made separately in units of size to fit my kiln conveniently, and all were carefully modelled to scale. The many parts were never assembled until actually set together in place in the prepared wall recess. In addition to the figures there were at least a hundred parts: modelled and glazed tiles for

[146]

background, for the well-head, the basin, the recess, the ornate corner of the well shelter, etc.

Leda, since she had to be fired in several pieces, was built and modelled as a unit. Then her head, arms and legs were cut off with a long thin blade in such a way as to give the most strength to the junction points where they were set together with cement in the final assembly.

Since none of the figures stands entirely free, the same assists were used in building the figures as in the final set-up. Leda leans on the well-head, and so she was built supported by a shelf of the right height. The other nude leans against a wall. The long neck of the swan is supported, so that no difficult problems were involved in the making of it.

Working in this piecemeal way demanded a thorough structural plan, but it gave me more freedom in the actual carrying out, more opportunities for re-doing and re-firing any unsatisfactory parts, than the small set for *Ten Nights in a Bar Room,* which was a one-piece structure.

I did Leda's torso over twice before I got one from the kiln to satisfy me; and I did her head three times.

The planning of the whole three-dimensional structure, the building of the recess with the basic forms of the well-head and the basin properly placed and proportioned to receive the tile, required a complete plan and a sense of structure, which I am sure most potters have.

For the water supply, soft lead pipes were used. They were easily bent into place, buried in the masonry, and punctured wherever spurts of water were wanted. Water comes into the well-head, flows through a spout into a small basin back of Leda, then falls into the main basin at the bottom. Along the inside of the outer rim of this basin runs a lead pipe from which a dozen thin sprays rise to drench the two nudes and the swan, and add to the sparkle of the glaze.

Complicated as this sculpture is, I do not believe there is any ceramic procedure or technique involved which has not been dealt with earlier in this chapter—only that to accomplish it you should be a carpenter, a mason and a tile-setter in addition to being a potter.

[147]

CHAPTER EIGHT

Slips, Glazes and Enamels

A SLIP OR ENGOBE is a thin coating of another clay applied over any ceramic ware to change its color. It should fire hard and permanent, but not fused, at the same temperature at which the ware is fired. If it fuses, it becomes a glaze.

A glaze is basically a coating of transparent glass over the ware. It is applied as finely ground powders, held in suspension in water, which fuse in the kiln. When a glaze is rendered opaque, most commonly through the presence of oxide of tin, it is called an enamel. Being opaque, enamels may be used over colored bodies, giving a positive color.

From the few formulas given at the end of this chapter you will see the close relationship of these three—slips, glazes and enamels—and will realize that they contain very much the same basic materials but in differing proportions. Clay mixed with water is a slip; add flux and it becomes a glaze; add an opacifier and it becomes an enamel.

Slips are generally light burning clays. Your primary problem is to make them stay permanently on the heavy body of your ware. Dark slips present less of a problem, for the clays used are more fusible and cling more tightly to an earthenware body.

Glazes and enamels are basically silica plus the necessary amount of flux to melt at the temperatures that are right for the proper maturing of the body. The primary problem here is the same: to make them fit your ware and stay on. Since they melt, they are much more positively attached to the body of the ware than are slips. If they are too fluid, they run off; and if not fluid enough, they tend to form into globules over the surface. To give them greater viscosity and body and to prevent them from running, a third element, alumina, is commonly added in the form of clay.

In their simplest terms both slips and glazes are very uncomplicated; and since a wide margin of error is not fatal, you should by all means start making and experimenting with your own.

The materials for glazes I accept as lying beyond my own personal contact more easily than I do the clays I use, but my attitude toward them is the same. Since I am only one person, I must accept the help of others in mining and burning and grinding and bringing together the various glaze components, but I keep those components as few in number as possible and as well known as possible. I use them with a sense of regret that they are so standardized, so purified, so perfect as to have lost all flavor of a place. And at every opportunity, I *add* local and unpredictable elements to them.

At Truro, on Cape Cod, where I have an old house, I find along the beach after some flood tides long windrows of a fine dark purple sand which I use in my slips for beautiful golden speckling. Back of a Gulf Coast beach in Florida I found milk-white sand, fine as dust, deposited by the wind, which with soda and a little flint gave me a fat but granular milky glaze that is beautiful with copper. From a sand bank where I go in New Jersey to get clay, I bring a rich burnt-orange sand, which in my slip gives a beautiful broken pink, fine for use as a heavy decorative engobe.

The thing most out of balance in present day amateur or hobby or educational or therapeutic or even one-man-factory potting is that the manual skill is often at a low, truly primitive level; the technical equipment at hand, however, is the product of advanced scientific knowledge. I think the only way to maintain health, both in the product and in the practitioners, is to start with all factors even. How much more fun it would be, and how much more interesting the results, if the clumsy things done in play schools or in institutions were decorated in other colored clays fired in an open fire, or in a stove or in simple kilns easily made! These things now, covered with a slick commercial glaze and fired in an electric kiln are certainly sick products of a sick civilization. Their permanence is horrible to think of! Imagine them unearthed 3,000 years from now to characterize the artistic impulses of the children of today. Compare them to the little toys which Chinese women and children of potters' families used to make and which you could buy for a few cents— some of them real masterpieces.

Making and Using Slips

The most foolproof slips are light burning ball clays. A light buff pipe clay has fine clinging properties and was the slip used in the Pennsylvania slip ware. If you want it whiter, add some china clay or kaolin; and if it then does not fire hard enough, add lead carbonate. Trial and error experimentation with your own clays is the only way to find your most satisfactory slip.

All the materials for your slips and glazes come to you finely ground. You can mix them thoroughly by passing them back and forth through a sixty-mesh sieve, grinding any coarse particles in a mortar by hand without much labor involved.

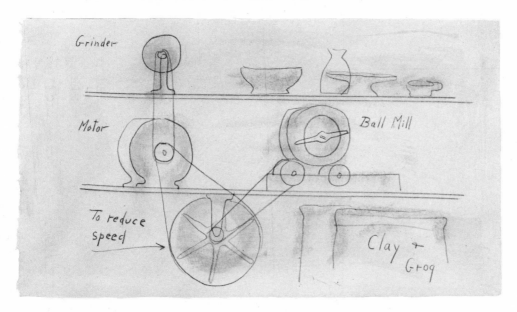

When I was starting pottery and getting what information I could from technical books, I became impressed by the importance of grinding my glazes. Having no electricity at that time to run a ball mill, but having a beautiful little stream at my kitchen door, I dammed the stream, set up an overshot water wheel, rigged up pulleys and rollers to turn my ball mill and happily set glaze batches grinding for hours on end—with disastrous results, for "crawling" glazes (those gathering into globules instead of lying flat over the ware) plagued me for years until I learned through this long hard discipline that coarsely ground glazes fit and lie flat much better than finely ground ones.

Now I have electricity and I use my one-gallon ball mill merely as the most convenient way of thoroughly mixing my glaze ingredients. I never grind them for more than forty-five minutes. So a ball mill is not a necessity, but some mortars are.

You should start keeping full and methodical notebooks to record your experiments. It has taken me years to realize how faulty my memory is; and some of my experiments which indicate directions which I would like to carry on, are so badly recorded as to be useless—a great waste of time.

The formulas for slips and glazes at the end of this chapter should

Ball Mill

serve only as points of departure into whatever you find most fits the clay you use, the temperatures you fire at and your own tastes.

To my taste, slips used very thinly are much preferable to heavy solid slips. First, they cling more solidly to the ware. A thick slip must have the same expansion and contraction as the base ware it covers, or it separates in time through the purely mechanical action of expanding and contracting as temperatures change in the use of the ware. A thin slip has not enough body to assert itself and push itself loose, even if it is slightly off perfection in this expansion and contraction process. Secondly, a thin slip, through which the color of the ground over which it is laid may show, gives more subtleties of variation, more pleasing conflicts between the two materials (slip and body), and is more fertile ground for the development of those infinitely intriguing qualities of the unpredictable which play such an important part in ceramics. In dealing with this you are on very delicate ground and may easily slip into artiness or affectation. Whatever is inherent in your method is apt to be good if you are a skillful workman. Ineptness and clumsiness can never be interesting in themselves and can only be tolerated if an exceptionally fresh and original idea shines through them.

In the use of slip as I have described it in the chapter on decoration, no binder is necessary; the adhesive character of the slip itself and its firm plastic quality (since it is mostly clay) hold it firmly until it is fired. With a glaze, however, the primary question may well be—how do you hold these water-suspended powders on the ware until they melt and fuse with the clay surface? Obviously there must be a binder of some sort.

In both slips and glazes, all the materials used are non-soluble in water; they are in suspension. (Soluble borax and soda can be used in a limited way, however, as I will describe later.) So in mixing and sieving or grinding you may use all the water you want and get rid of the excess by allowing it to settle or evaporate or be absorbed in a porous container, without loss of any of the glaze materials. But if you use a water-soluble gum or glue of any sort as a binder, you may lose an undetermined part of your binder with any excess water you get rid of. Therefore the simplest procedure, I find, is to thicken your glaze batch, even let it dry out completely in a large open container, and add the binder to each batch as you add water to thin it for use. You can sprinkle some powdered gum arabic into it as you mix, or in thinning use water already holding enough gum tragacanth to thicken or slightly coagulate it. Both these gums are very mild adhesives.

You should use as little of them as necessary to hold. Too much will make your glaze shrink and crack in drying. A teaspoon of powdered gum arabic to half a gallon of glaze is enough for my glazes. I dissolve a tablespoonful of powdered gum tragacanth in a gallon of water and keep this for use in bringing all dry glazes to a fluid state.

Using Glazes and Enamels

For use with sgraffito and all underglaze decoration, a satisfactory clear glaze is most important. It is quite simple to mix a good *raw glaze* which does not need any previously fritted materials. When you have one that fits your ware and your taste and your temperatures, you are very well off, for that can be the basic formula to which you add tin for a white enamel; vary the proportions of spar and flint to get more matte or more glossy surfaces; and add the metallic oxides for colors. Lead carbonate (dry white lead) is the most useful flux, and short of constant exposure to it in industrial plants you do not need to worry over its poisonous properties.

Lead has its own influence on the color your oxides will give, as do soda, borax and potash; but for earthenware and all temperatures below stoneware, where the potash of feldspar becomes your flux, lead is generally the most easy and satisfactory to use.

If glazes and enamels interest you more than form and decoration, you will certainly be led into many experiments with other fluxes, particularly with soda, for the magnificent blues which you get from copper, and the rich purples from manganese dioxide. Both soda and borax are water soluble; and so if you go seriously into their use, you must be prepared to undertake the very considerable business of fritting and grinding. This has always kept me from more than nibbling at their use, as a sort of hit and miss alchemy not to be depended on and in fact calling for not only more time than I can give, but calling more attention to itself than I feel it deserves.

A few Persian-blue goblets which I had on my shelves would draw exclamations of wonder from visitors, to the complete neglect of fine form, decoration, subtle color and surface quality on other pieces. But the rich fat glazes and glowing color of Persian pottery—all attained with basically soda fluxes—were certainly worth many pains to attain.

I glaze almost all my work by pouring, in the way I have described for slipping. I vary the thickness of the glaze by a glaze mix, the thickness or diluteness of which is adjusted to the absorbent quality of what it is to be poured over. All these operations which I would like to make exact for the reader's sake seem very inexact as I write them down, but I hope they give a starting point. Only endless trial and error can carry them beyond that.

When you have finished a beautiful decoration, as on a plate for instance, with delicate and exact lines and color areas, it seems as you flood the glaze over it that you have lost everything. But even the mildest binder which you may have used with your oxide colors holds them

exactly if your slip or clay ground is absorbent, since the first flow of glaze is held stationary, while the subsequent flow is added to the top of it. If the glaze is so thick that it flows in the fire, then it shifts your colors and lines—except for sgraffito lines which hold exactly even under a flowing glaze.

As I glaze decorated plates and bowls I vary the fusing point of the glaze in a very inexact and rule-of-thumb way, roughly calculated for things to be set either on the kiln bottom (the hottest part) or on the middle or top; and I set them on shelves corresponding to their future position in the kiln. For the mid-kiln, I use my standard raw lead glaze calculated to be at its clear best at cone 05. For the bottom ware I add sometimes chalk (whiting), sometimes spar, sometimes leached wood ash from my fireplace, in guesswork quantities. For the top, I add borax or soda, both soluble, to my ready glaze mix. Both these fluxes permeate the slip and help hold it to the ware, as well as exert a tendency to burn the slip away; they also influence the colors. All these variables produce, as you can imagine, different results; and for standardized use they would have to be reduced to exact measurements. But for my use and the constant excitement of new discoveries, surprisingly wide variations still give results which, even in the failures, may open directions that invite me to follow.

It is clear that interest in glazes can lead into great complications which call for exact chemical knowledge, for much technical equipment, and most of all for abreast-of-the-moment information on all materials available through modern industry and technology.

Glazes are the last refinement of pottery, and a knowledge and use of glazes throughout the history of pottery came only after great achievement in the beautiful and expressive use of clay had been reached, when form and decoration in themselves had great eloquence. Then the discovery and use of glazes, while it made pottery certainly much more useful and practical, shifted the emphasis away from pure form into the more superficial charm of color and texture—or into the purely practical and utilitarian. Even the incomparable Chinese porcelains of the Sung period are notably weaker, more feminine in form, than the earlier sturdy and magnificent pots, urns and jugs that preceded them back into the very dawn of man. The fat, rich, alkaline glazes of the Persians weakened the forms and emasculated the designs of their desert-born predecessors, the early Assyrians. We can be thankful that the Cretans, Greeks and Etruscans never discovered glazes; neither did the Peruvians, Mayans and early Mexicans.

A recognition of these things poses the most serious problem for the contemporary potter who brings to his work his highest aspirations and ideals. Can simplicity and the virtues of uncomplicated directness in doing and expressing be kept in a complicated technological age? For myself and for this moment in the writing of this book, my best answer is to stick to the really elementary things, to acquire skill in the use of these elementary things and faith in their sufficiency when you feel that through them you have attained real expressive eloquence.

Since I would like to have in this book *everything* you need to know in making beautiful pottery, at the end of the book I will add for the technical-minded a bibliography of works dealing more fully with the technical aspects of potting.

Some Formulas

Weights in the following formulas are, of course, simply ratios and can be stated in grams or ounces or pounds. Mine are in terms of BB shot, because I acquired an old pair of grocer's balances but no weights. Having by chance a supply of BB shot, I melted them into flat pellets in units of five, which gave me much finer divisions of weight than are really necessary. In starting I was much more in awe of these niceties than I am now.

I enter these few formulas direct from my record book. You can divide these large figures by ten or whatever number proves convenient. For example, 2760 represents about three pounds, and this amount of white lead with the other ingredients *in proportion* makes a good load for my one-gallon ball mill.

No. 1—Clear Raw Lead Glaze

2760	White lead	560	Flint
180	Whiting	220	Cornwall stone
960	Spar	60	Oxide of zinc
240	Kaolin		

This is a clear, colorless, fat glaze with a firing range from 07 to 02. At 02, when used thickly, it runs but does not burn off. It is excellent on sgraffito and over underglaze decoration. You may color it by small or large quantities of metallic oxides. Since I work almost entirely over slips, I prefer to put color in the slip. I do often add about 100 parts tin to this formula, or even less, with some color, for a semi-opaque colored glaze.

No. 2—For higher temperatures, from 04 to 2, I increase the ratios of whiting and spar:

2760	White lead	600	Flint
210	Whiting	160	China clay
1400	Spar	60	Zinc oxide
240	Kaolin		

No. 3—For a more matte surface, but still showing underglaze decoration and sgraffito sharply, I have used this at cone 03 to 3:

4000	White lead	200	Flint
1000	Whiting	350	Pipe clay
3700	Spar	300	Zinc oxide
950	China clay		

As for the amount of coloring oxide to be effective in a glaze, cobalt is most powerful and consequently is used more sparingly than any other of the metals. Here is a formula stated in grams (as it was given to me by a fellow potter) for a very fine gray which indicates how and in what ratio colors may be balanced against each other (cone 04; quite matte):

35	White lead	3.5	Ball clay
10	Whiting	2	Flint
37	Spar	.4	Manganese dioxide
3	Zinc oxide	.3	Manganese carbonate
9.5	China clay	.1	Cobalt oxide

My record book is full of countless experimental and changing formulas, most of which represent purely wasted energy and time, but I could not have been satisfied if I had not tried them.

I use red lead principally for enamels (cone 04 to 07):

460	Red lead	150	China clay
920	White lead	270	Tin
115	Whiting	30	Zinc oxide
300	Spar	100	Kaolin
200	Flint		

For a very rich, fine black here are two formulas (cone 02 to 08):

460	Red lead	500	Blue Haverstraw clay
920	White lead	50	Black iron oxide
115	Whiting	50	Black manganese
100	Tin	50	Manganese dioxide
100	Spar	25	Black cobalt oxide
100	Flint		

[159]

Another:

2760	Red lead	100	Black manganese
300	Whiting	50	Manganese dioxide
200	Spar	25	Black cobalt
200	Flint	200	Leached wood ash
1000	Haverstraw clay	100	Crocus martis
100	Black iron oxide		

Crocus martis is a dark red iron oxide. The wood ash serves as an opacifier and prevents flowing. For Haverstraw clay you can, of course, substitute any clay rich in iron, or Albany slip.

As a starting point I will list a few mixtures—you could scarcely call them formulas—which I have tried for soda and borax glazes to use with copper for turquoise blue. They are measured, ground by hand in a mortar with more than normal binder (powdered gum tragacanth or gum arabic), put through a thirty-mesh sieve and used immediately, preferably by pouring and preferably on biscuited ware. On raw ware, the soda and borax, being in solution, penetrate the ware and often cause large flakes to shale off in firing.

(Cone 05):

300	Soda ash	25	China clay
225	Flint	75	Cornwall stone
100	Zinc oxide	5	Black oxide of copper

(Cone 06):

300	Soda ash	100	Spar
100	Borax	25	Tin
50	China clay	7	Black copper
100	Flint	2	Black cobalt

[160]

In any of these glaze formulas, you can replace Cornwall stone with the same quantity of feldspar. The spars you get from different sources will vary somewhat, but not greatly.

As you fire at higher temperatures, you can lessen the amount of lead and increase that of whiting and spar, and with these variables work toward shiny or matte glazes. At high temperatures—those for stoneware, china and porcelain—glazes can discard lead entirely, since the potash in feldspar serves as a flux.

I have tried and still do try innumerable variations in slips, to vary color, texture, and suitability for the different bodies I use, and for resistance or susceptibility to burning off under any glazes.

First, try straight pipe clay as you get it from a dealer; it gives a smooth, well-clinging cream-colored slip. Try mixing with it any yellow sand which would pass through a forty-sieve.

To make a whiter slip:

200	China clay	200	Spar
200	Pipe clay	200	White lead

At high temperatures this melts and becomes a glaze. Up to that point it is a white slip.

If you want a cool white, add a tiny bit of cobalt sulphate to your slip. It serves the same purpose as adding blueing to your wash, in that it counteracts the yellowish tendency.

Another slip:

200	China clay	80	Ball clay
200	Pipe clay	100	White lead
200	Spar	50	Borax

None of the slips needs to be ground. They can be mixed dry; then reduced to creamy consistency and sieved back and forth through several sieves of constantly finer mesh. I often add the borax—the water soluble element—at the very end, after which I pass the whole mix through only a coarse sieve. Then I use the slip immediately. The coarse, undissolved particles of borax, distributed through the slip, give a speckling where they fuse in the fire under the glaze. This is not only a pleasant breaking of the uniform surface, but it also helps greatly in the secure attachment between slip and body.

If you are using a light buff burning clay, it is well to include some of it in your slip. In the mixture above substitute it for your pipe clay and ball clay. It helps in the secure attachment to the body.

Dark slips present no difficulties. They can carry a great deal of plastic fusible clay which clings securely to your ware. There is on the market a clay rich in manganese and iron called Blackbird clay, which I use with Haverstraw clay for black slips. To this I add more black iron, manganese for darker tints, and some black cobalt for a really complete black.

The combinations I use are so variable that I have never even recorded them by exact weight, but this formula will indicate general proportions:

400	*Haverstraw clay—*	*20*	*Black manganese*
	or any low firing red	*20*	*Crocus martis*
	burning clay you have.	*10*	*Manganese dioxide*
100	*Blackbird clay*	*5*	*Cobalt oxide*

Dark slips, being quite thin, cover well and go a long way. Glazes and enamels when applied heavily are used up much more rapidly. With so many variables it is impossible to state how much you will need for any given work. When you make any glaze or slip—except for the most unsure, most experimental—make about a quart, for in dipping or pouring it is good to have a liberal quantity to work from.

CHAPTER NINE

❦

Kilns

IN OUR WORLD there are the known and the unknown. To my earth-bound temperament the known has always been much more enchanting than the unknown. That is why I hate gadgets with concealed workings, where you press a button and unknown springs and wheels and forces do something for you. I like to see the wheels and springs and forces working. I like a curtain hung on big rings sliding on a rod, and I can't abide those wooden tubes with a concealed spring that roll the curtain up for you.

Of course the most known, most obvious, most tangible is full of the unknown, and the awareness of this may be much of the reason for the enchantment of the known. For the eyes and for the hands the known has so much of the miraculous that when the mind also dwells on it, the complications quickly become so great as to confuse the clarity and directness of use that are important in the creation of a work of art. I believe that in all the arts of construction—all those that use materials and depend upon the character of the material for a large part of the character of the finished work, such as architecture, pottery, sculpture, even painting—the utmost style, or elegance, is achieved through this appreciation of and delight in the obvious, the unconcealed, the basically known.

There is no doubt that the "known" is an entirely variable quality, quite different for persons of different temperament and training and environment, but in thinking of creativity in the arts of construction, I have great faith in the norm, the continually repeated average of human experience. The things that change and have changed in our external world during the development of our scientific and technical age have certainly modified this norm, but only in ways which I think can justly be called superficial when weighed with the continuing basic contacts of our lives.

In my house I have a big open fireplace, and the direct heat from blazing logs gives me a pleasure not to be found in however hot a radiator. The flame in an open, gas-burning heater is no substitute, while the glow of an incandescent coil in an electric heater is as nothing. The burning logs are tangible, the living flames that consume them are "known," are familiar; but, heaven knows, the process you are watching and which holds you enchanted, is more miraculous, more stimulating to the imagination than the heat of an electric oven.

The wonder of this miracle of fire is as old and as basic to the race as the instinct for survival. Before your eyes those solid, heavy logs become flame and smoke, become apparently weightless energy and heat. I agree that the sudden incandescent light and heat which result from the turning of an electric switch is equally miraculous, but cause and effect are so remote, so hidden, that they soon are put into that ever-growing category of things taken for granted, things intangible and dehumanizing like the transmission of sounds over radio and of sights over television. I believe that through this the sense of wonder which is so basic a factor in creative communication is lessened, and correspondingly the sensuous richness so vital in the arts of construction is tragically weakened.

Strangely enough, fire is never taken for granted. It may charm and comfort you, or terrify you, but it is always alive. It is bound up with the creative and the experimental, the unpredictable which has been and must always be of the essence in the creative art of pottery. When the product becomes standardized, when similarity and repetition become the desired end, when art has departed from the ceramic industry, then it naturally follows that standardized heat becomes the most desirable.

I write this to find the reasons for my faith in a wood-burning kiln, but perhaps it isn't reasonable. It may be simply that because I was brought up with wood- and coal-burning stoves and furnaces, I understand drafts and flues and take pleasure in clean combustion; that I built fireplaces before I ever built kilns; and that I know nothing about electricity. So it may be reasonable only for me, and perhaps only some remnants of a puritanical and missionary conceit urge me to believe it to be sound and healthy and basic. But at any rate, I do believe it, and urge every young potter to try it, and so I will include here some simple and practical plans of kilns I have built and used.

My Workshop and Kilns

In trying to give as practical assistance and advice as possible, it may be helpful now for me to give you the plan of my pottery and outdoor clay yard. My present workshop is the third and, I hope, the final expansion

of my potting. I first built my wheel and started work in a corner of my large painting studio in 1921. I was set to build a kiln when a friend who had tried and abandoned pottery gave me a small, round Revelation oil-burning kiln which I hooked into the house furnace flue. The excessive heat soon cracked and endangered the furnace flue; so off my studio I built a small room for a pottery with its own flue for the kiln.

PLAN OF POTTERY AND YARD

1 *Wheel; windows on both sides.*

2 *Stove, with drying cabinet and shelves.*

3 *Big drawing table.*

4 *Work counters with grinding wheel and glaze grinder.*

5 *Concrete work table.*

6 *Clay bins with cover at counter height.*

7 *Sink.*

8 *Glaze counter: shelves over; clay tubs under.*

9 *Concrete platform with two Revelation kilns.*

10 *Cabinet for finished ware. Tiers of shelves to ceiling.*

11 *Stairway down into studio.*

12 *Open lean-to over kiln and wood and clay tubs.*

13 *Wood burning kiln.*

14 *Concrete work table.*

15 *Coal and coke kiln.*

16 *Windows; also skylight over wheel and over work table (5).*

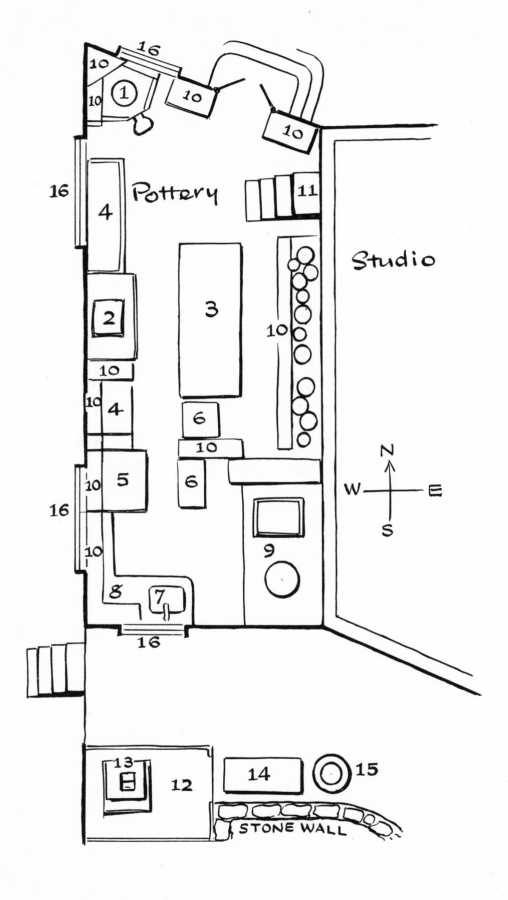

In this Revelation kiln, with a round fourteen-inch muffle, I fired all my work for three years, and in using it acquired my excessive regard for economy of space in stacking. Then at the start (though it is also true now) so much of my work was experimental that the use of a small kiln was very sensible. If you ruin everything in a firing you have lost only a few days' work. This kiln has been a marvel. With several rebuildings with more refractory materials, it has lasted through hundreds of firings and is still ready for work that must be turned out on short notice.

After three years with increasing sale of work, I bought a larger Revelation kiln with an 18x22-inch muffle, and in this an astonishing amount of work can be packed. For simplicity of firing and durability these kilns are excellent. The bottom gets much hotter than the top, but I learned to take advantage of this variation. The big kiln, heavily loaded, I bring up to cone 05 slowly, seven to eight hours or longer; then cap the flue, stop the drafts and allow twelve hours for cooling. You must have at least fifteen feet of stack to induce a strong draft and avoid sooting up. Kerosene burns with a long flame which at the end of a firing is leaping three feet out of the chimney top. There is still great fuel economy—never more than ten gallons to a firing, which at sixteen cents a gallon makes the manufacturing costs trifling.

After ten years' work in my first small, crowded room, I built my present pottery in 1931. Fourteen by twenty-two feet, it is none too large since I accumulate junk and am not a tidy workman; if it were twice as large, it would be equally full. Aside from the main fixtures shown on the plan, I have shelving everywhere up to the low ceiling; skylights over the wheel and glazing spaces, as well as many windows; while for summer my open clay yard is a pleasant extension of space.

For working tables—beating clay, glazing, everything—build a very solid table to fit the space you want with a four-inch deep trough for a top. In the trough lay some irons and wire for reinforcing, and pour it full of concrete. Finish the top inch with a one-to-two mix of cement and fine sand, and after it has set several hours, polish hard and thoroughly with a plasterer's trowel. If you catch it at the right time, just before setting, you can get a beautiful and almost indestructible surface. On this table I keep several heavy plaster slabs for wedging and stiffening clay, and from the ceiling hangs a wire which I hook under the front of my table for cutting. This saves a separate wedging table and enables me, by changing slabs, to vary the absorbing character of the plaster for different work.

It was not until 1950, on my return from a year in Italy, where I had been freshly intrigued by the simplicity of the kilns turning out the native pottery, that I built my own wood-burning kiln. I also had the itch to try again some copper reds. Twenty years before, with crucibles sunk in the coals of my house furnace, I had got some magnificent transparent scarlet reds. The half dozen perfect goblets which were the result of months of experimenting sold readily at high prices, but I had taken myself in hand with the question: "Is this what you want to spend your life doing? It's a lifetime job." So I quit flat, keeping only one broken goblet as a record. Now finding this goblet after twenty years, I felt more leisurely and more patient, and I needed the relaxation of doing some building. This itch to build is a recurrent need, coming with the spring.

Upon finishing this first kiln and firing it once with complete success, I built another at our summer school at Skowhegan,* with the students helping. This we have used with entire success for ceramic sculpture. Students continuing their work elsewhere with electric kilns have greatly missed the fine variations and flame discolorations which we have in the open kiln.

In the plans which follow, common fire brick is used; but the sculptor Charles Rudy, who was at Skowhegan, has very successfully built a kiln on this plan with insulating bricks. These are soft and can be cut and shaped much more easily than regular fire brick. The arches, however, should be built of the most strong and refractory brick you can get.

---

* The Skowhegan School of Painting and Sculpture, Skowhegan, Maine.

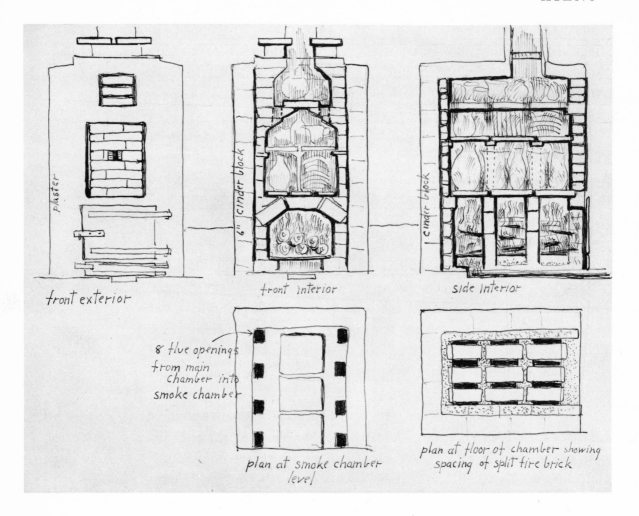

front exterior

front interior

side interior

8 flue openings
from main
chamber into
smoke chamber

plan at smoke chamber
level

plan at floor of chamber showing
spacing of split fire brick

Stacking

In stacking the open kiln you must have some regard for the travelling
of the flame up through the ware, but if you have seen the close setting
of bricks in the old open flame kilns you will realize that the flame will
find its way upward through small and devious ways. What is important

[170]

is to give it near the bottom enough space and air not to choke the flame down too quickly, or you will burn the bottom pieces unduly before the top comes up to heat. The kiln itself is the flue, and as it heats, the pull gets more and more fierce. Only enough flue over the kiln is needed to carry the sparks and flame away from your shed roof.

For sculpture and unglazed ware almost no shelving is needed, for pieces can be set against and on one another to a considerable height with due regard for diminishing weight and strength as you build up. A few tall props and light shelving help make a solid structure. A big variety of shapes and sizes is good to have, but it calls for ingenuity in the setting.

With glazed ware you stack as you would in a muffle kiln. Saggers can, of course, be used; but do not be afraid to trust your most delicate ware to the open flame. Or, should I say, reserve them for a muffle kiln, and fire only sturdy pieces in the flame. I would not venture to advise anyone on setting a kiln, as I have discovered in the few times when I have seen other settings (except in careless Italy) that I am too unortho- dox, too stingy of space, and too risky. But nevertheless, I very often have 100 per cent perfect firings, as far as cracking is concerned.

Plates I stack like this to a height often of seven or eight, being careful to have the bearing points of the stilts over each other as much as possible.

Bowls like this:

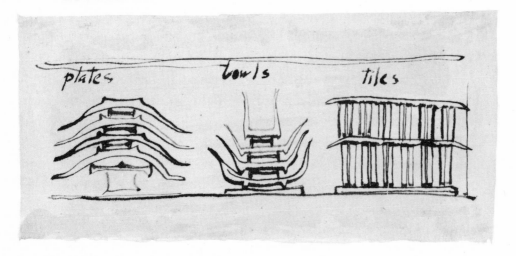

Tiles like this: Back to back with two clay rolls laid over the top and slightly squeezed down between the glazed surfaces to keep them ¼- to ½-inch apart, and often several tiers high. If there is a little warping, what matter? Leave uniformity and technical perfection to the factories. St. Mark's mosaicists realized what is gained by the breaking up of surfaces through irregular setting of the tisserae. Don't think they could not have made them regular and even.

Firing

My most disastrous kiln accidents have been caused by pieces exploding from imprisoned steam and showering every glazed piece in the kiln with large and small flakes. Now I am led into that error only through some desperately hurried job—or more honestly, perhaps, sheer greediness in wanting to see how something comes out without waiting the allotted drying time. So to guard against this undue hurry I generally follow this procedure:

With the shelves by my kiln full of more than enough ware to give plenty of choice in setting and filling every odd space, I pack the kiln in late afternoon. This must be done in relaxed leisure. Then in the oil-fired kiln I start a low drip fire which I let go all night for slow final drying of both clay and glazes and kiln, increasing it in early morning and finishing about noon or early afternoon.

At Skowhegan with the heavy wood-burning kiln we do the same. We start a very small fire in the late afternoon. The students stay up late to tend it and are most insistent on keeping it very low. The fire is banked and the flues closed around midnight. In the morning the drafts are opened and new fuel fed in, which finishes it off about three or four o'clock in the afternoon, with flames roaring out all six of the flues—a quite awesome business. The amount of wood required is surprisingly small, although through the middle period of bringing it up to red heat a good roaring fire is necessary. For finishing off we throw in bundles of edging from a local sawmill.

KILNS

At home I make faggots of light twigs and split wood for finishing. When such a bundle six inches in diameter is fed into the fire box and falls apart as the cord burns, so much surface is exposed to combustion that the result is practically an explosion, and I wonder how the ware inside survives. The scorching heat from the fire box calls for good heavy asbestos gloves on the fireman's hands.

In placing your pyrometric cones, be very sure that for clear vision they are accurately lined up with the spy hole. One group of two or three should be near the back; the other toward the front of the kiln. The advantage of bricking up the front, over closing it with a solid door, is that you can vary the position of the spy hole up or down, to suit your packing. The right temperatures for maturing the native Maine clays we use are 08 to 06, but we must be sure that the things on the bottom are of the most refractory clays.

For high temperatures and experiments in reducing I built this small round kiln to duplicate somewhat the conditions through which I got my first handsome copper reds.

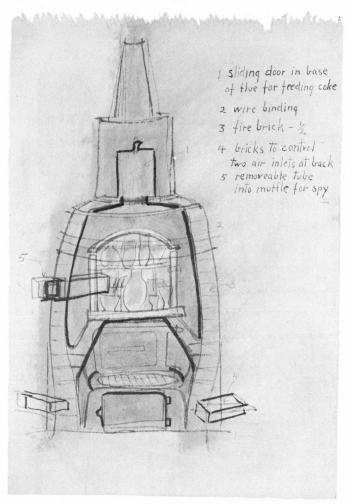

1 sliding door in base of flue for feeding coke
2 wire binding
3 fire brick - ½
4 bricks to control two air inlets at back
5 removeable tube into muffle for spy

On the permanent floor I can set a round sagger with a lid and so have a muffle kiln. Or I can set open shelving, and fire in the direct flame. I load it from the top, then set the top ring and flue in place. When I use the sagger, I can finish off by feeding fuel into the top through a door in the chimney, which enables me to surround the whole muffle with coke at an incandescent heat. This, starting with wood and coal, then coke, I fire in about four hours to cone 4 or 5. Through the same door in the big base of the chimney through which I feed fuel, I slide clay slabs partially or entirely over the opening in the top ring to get any amount of reduction I want.

In this kiln I have got some very handsome reds—as well as many black, blistered failures. Always after several firings, working with these miraculous but for me always unpredictable reds, I go back with relief to the simple techniques more entirely under my control; then am drawn back again to those elusive scarlets with all the subtle purples and mauves and smoky grays that sometimes reward even the failures. Anyway, the perfect reds are dull and uninteresting.

A Wood-Burning Kiln

The proportions of this kiln were determined by the size of the units in its construction—standard fire brick 4½x2½x9 inches. Bricks were set edgewise and laid up with six-inch cinderblocks outside for strength and insulation.

The rather wide joint between the inner fire brick and the outer shell of cinderblock is loosely packed with asbestos fibre and sand with an occasional solid tie of mortar, along each course. The chamber is 18 inches (two fire bricks) wide, by 27 inches (three fire bricks) long. Supported by the two arches over the fire box and projecting brick at back and front, split fire bricks are fitted snugly end to end, with 1½ inches open space between the sides. "Split" fire brick is a standard brick 4¼x 1¼x8½ inches. Some cutting and shaping must be done for the arches and for drawing in the top of the main chamber and smoke chamber.

First experimental goblets for copper reds, by H. V. Poor

The eight flues, about 2½x2½ inches, leading from the sides of the chamber into the smoke chamber insure an even heat spread. The smoke chamber may be packed with ware to be biscuited.

Two lengths of 7-x7-inch square flue lining carry the flame and sparks above my lean-to roof. The terra cotta flue lining I wrap with metal lath, and plaster it thickly with a lime and cement mortar carrying, along with sand, a third part of asbestos fibre. At the base of the flue I have two sliding fire brick slabs to control the draft for reducing.

Under the ash pit I have a long strip of sheet steel, covering a flat channel leading to the back of the pit, for an air inlet. This draws the flame forward, as the front of the kiln is harder to heat than the back.

The main chamber and the smoke chamber after loading are closed by bricks bedded in dry fire clay. The opening into the main chamber is one and one-half bricks wide; the smoke chamber opening, one brick wide. The bricks are clearly numbered and fit snugly so that the closing and taking down with each firing is not at all an arduous job. Here they are, of course, set flat, not edgewise.

The fire bricks are laid in Johns-Manville refractory fire clay No. 32.

Somewhat more than halfway up in the walls of the chamber I have set projecting spurs of brick to carry shelving. The shelving should be very open to allow free passage of the flame.

After one or two firings some cracks are sure to develop through the whole kiln, but if your arches are laid up by over-hanging brick rather than by a keyed arch you do not need to worry. Our kiln at Skowhegan had arched brick over the chamber, and after half a dozen firings we had to band the kiln to stop its spreading. A look at the plan of the New City kiln will show that only the fire pit arches exert any side thrust, and these are practically at ground level—side and back—as the kiln is built into a bank.

The front of the kiln is plastered heavily with an insulating plaster to compensate for its lack of cinderblock protection. The inside has a heavy wash of fire clay and flint.

CHAPTER TEN

❧

Practical Helps and Definitions

THE USE OF CLAY and the development and refinements of the whole art of pottery making come from such remote antiquity, and so much precede any corresponding development of the exact sciences, which might codify and explain what went on in the fire and what caused these transformations, that the aura of mystery and of the unknown and miraculous has always enveloped pottery making. Trade secrets have played quite a part in ceramic manufacture and do even to the present time. Let us hope that to some extent they always will, for they represent the entirely personal and human element, the procedures that make one man's way of doing different from another's. To realize that there are many things common to human beings, which are still too subtle for chemical analysis, is to me a source of comfort. For ex-

[176]

ample, I have never found any dyes as fast as those made by the German dye works before the first World War, and the chemically reproduced flavors of cheeses fail sadly to equal the originals.

In the ceramic industry, as chemical analysis and processes have isolated and refined the materials used, the "artist-potters" have been kept busy putting the impurities back or consciously imitating imperfections of more primitive work.

[177]

This is not peculiar to our times. The Chinese, even in their most productive periods such as the Ming and later dynasties, devoted part of their production to a conscious imitation and preservation of earlier ware. Such sensibilities are in our time ruled out of industry and relegated to the very fringes of our society, to the antiquarians or the "arty," who protest in vain as landmark after landmark in our cities is pulled down to make room for bigger returns on the investment.

In 1921 when I started doing pottery there were very few manuals on how-to-do-it. Now there are many, and some are very good indeed; so to supplement the many omissions in this book you may consult the brief bibliography at the end of Chapter Eight. In my own experience, when I tried to supplement my trial-and-error education by research and reading, I met technical treatises beyond my understanding, or descriptions of processes containing so many gaps that I concluded trade secrecy was still dominant.

My "trial-and-error" education was most limited, most painful, because it started with myself. If I had had any holdovers from other workers, other traditions, they would have been a great help; but there are times—and my own mood was to think that this was one of them— when one feels that all close preceding traditions had better be ignored.

In this final chapter I will, however, try to bring together and explain fundamental terms, methods, and practical helps which I may have overlooked or taken for granted so far in the book.

Cones

One of the first and most important aids in taking the uncertainties of temperature out of the firing process was the development and use of pyrometric cones. These are three-inch long slender cones made of mixtures of clays and fluxes combined in accurately measured quantities to melt and fall over at given temperatures. They are graded by differences of about twenty degrees all the way from 022, a dull red heat, 605

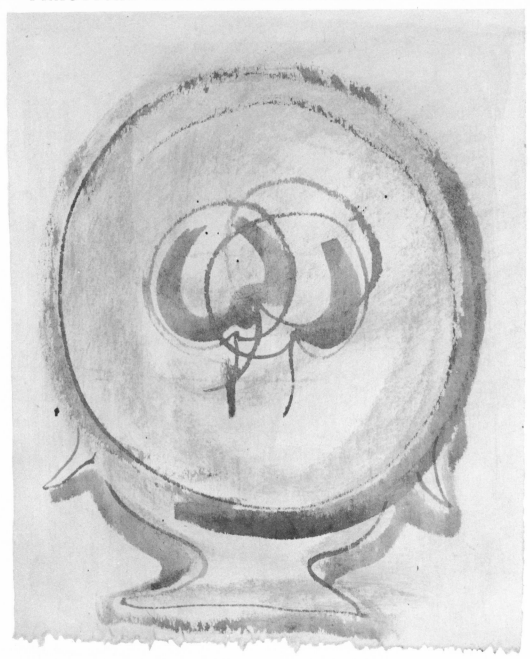

centigrade, to 15, which melts at the incandescent heat of 2600 for porcelain. These, placed where they can be watched through the spy hole, are much more accurate than judgments of color, which must have been the only guide of the early potter.

[179]

SCALE

CONE	CENTIGRADE	FAHRENHEIT	
022	605	1121	*Dehydration takes place.*
021	615	1139	
020	650	1202	
019	660	1220	
018	720	1328	
017	770	1418	*Any organic matter in clay*
016	798	1463	*burns out.*
015	805	1481	
014	830	1526	
013	860	1580	
012	875	1607	*Lustre glazes and low fire*
011	895	1643	*overglaze colors.*
010	905	1661	
09	930	1706	
08	950	1742	
07	990	1814	
06	1015	1859	*Red earthenware and low*
05	1040	1904	*fire lead glazes. Majolica*
04	1060	1940	*glazes. Tin enamels.*
03	1115	2039	
02	1125	2057	*Buff clays. Earthware.*
01	1145	2093	
1	1160	2120	
2	1165	2129	
3	1170	2138	*Low fire stoneware.*
4	1190	2174	
5	1205	2201	
6	1230	2246	

CONE	CENTIGRADE	FAHRENHEIT	
7	1250	2282	*Stoneware and salt glazes.*
8	1260	2300	
9	1285	2345	
10	1305	2381	*China.*
11	1325	2417	
12	1335	2435	
13	1350	2462	*Porcelain.*
14	1400	2552	
15	1435	2615	

Solution VERSUS Suspension

You must distinguish between something in *solution* in water and something in *suspension*. Sugar and salt are in solution in water. They cannot be filtered out, but will pass through any filter as liquid. They do separate through evaporation. Almost all the materials for glazes are non-soluble—are carried in suspension—and can be filtered out. *Borax* and *soda* are soluble in water, and so their use with non-soluble ingredients is difficult and uncertain. The *mineral oxides* used for colors in glazes are non-soluble, but those same minerals as *salts* are soluble in water, and in this form are very useful as stains which develop their color as the glaze fluxes.

Frits and Fritting

You can handle soda and borax best by mixing them dry with other glaze ingredients, melting this mixture and then regrinding the melted glass. This is called *fritting,* and the insoluble powder which results can be held in suspension with other glaze materials and applied over the ware.

[181]

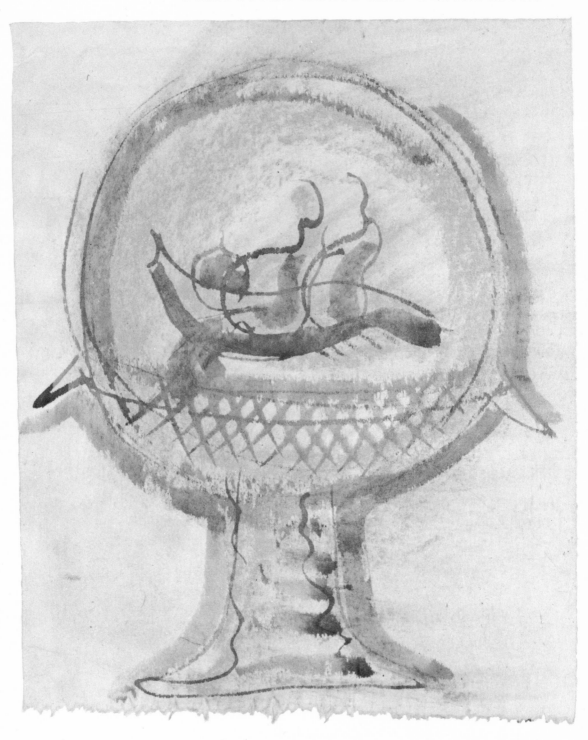

Most high fire glazes in industrial use, where perfect smoothness is important, have some proportion of fritted material.

Raw glazes are glazes using no previously fritted materials.

A *slip* or *engobe* is clay thinned in water to whatever consistency the intended use demands. Its common use is as a thin coating over any clay body to change its color. In general the light burning clays, maturing at high temperatures, have little shrinkage and do not adhere as firmly to the earthenware bodies which they cover as do slips made from the plastic red burning clays. I make a black slip from Haverstraw blue clay with varied proportions of manganese, cobalt, and black iron oxide added.

Metallic Oxides for Color in Slips or Glazes

Iron comes as a black or red oxide and gives a great variety of color from red to black to bluish gray depending upon firing conditions. Under a reducing flame it gives celadon-green grays. It gives its brightest red-browns with an oxidizing flame and at low temperatures. It burns out at high temperatures.

Cobalt is a black powder, the most indestructible and positive of blues, holding at all temperatures and all firing conditions.

Copper comes as a black or dull red powder. Most commonly it gives a green. With soda flux it gives a turquoise blue. Under certain reducing flames it gives reds.

Manganese comes in black powders. The oxides give dark greens and blacks. The dioxide gives purple and purplish browns.

[183]

Antimony, a white oxide, gives pale yellow.

Uranium, a dull orange powder, gives stronger yellows.

Chrome gives a dull green, and at low temperatures rather bad, hard, bright reds.

Tin, a white oxide, stays a clear white in suspension in the glaze. It gives a white enamel which can, of course, be stained by any of the other metals, while the white of the tin serves as the foil to lighten and brighten their color.

Zinc white oxide melts in a glaze and gives extra clearness and brilliance to a transparent glaze.

Titanium, a white oxide, acts somewhat as tin, but is much less powerful.

Lead-white, or lead carbonate, is the most powerful flux. Red lead or white lead is equally powerful. Lead gives a slightly yellowish tinge to a glaze.

Gold and silver are of use only as colors or lusters at very low temperatures. When china or porcelain carries gold in its decoration, it is fired on after the body and glaze have been previously fired.

Ball clays are plastic sedimentary clays which have escaped with little iron, and so fire quite light in color. They often have picked up much organic matter and are stained sometimes almost black from the carbon of decaying bogs, which burns out in the firing. They are very useful in mixing with china clay and kaolin to give plasticity to white bodies; also in white slips.

A *reducing* flame is the product of incomplete combustion. The

gases being shy of oxygen, rob any of the metallic oxides in the kiln of any oxygen they can get. In doing this they make some startling color changes. In the case of copper, they turn green into red.

An *oxidizing* flame is one plentifully supplied with oxygen. It develops the clear normal color of the metallic oxides.

I have omitted here a Glossary of Terms, as this seems to me unnecessary, since I have used so few technical terms.

For other omissions, notably material dealing with mould-making and casting, I offer no apology. These omissions are part of the obvious bias of the book—a bias stemming from my deep dislike of the gadgetry and packaging and mass production with which we are surrounded.

I have attempted to deal only with my own practices; but since in practice I am a trial-and-error workman and not very methodical in documenting even my most successful results, my readers will find that this book has many shortcomings on the technical side. Perhaps these are the necessary foil for what merit the book may have in other directions.

BIBLIOGRAPHY

Binns, C. F., *The Potter's Craft*. Princeton, N. J.: Van Nostrand, 1947. A good manual.

"Ceramics," *Encyclopaedia Britannica*. A very excellent general historical and technical treatise.

Cox, George J., *Pottery*. New York: Macmillan, 1914. General manual.

Kenny, John B., *Ceramic Sculpture*. New York: Greenberg, 1953. Practical and helpful.

Kenny, John B., *Complete Book of Pottery Making*. New York: Greenberg, 1949. All that its name implies.

Leach, Bernard, *A Potter's Book*. London: Faber & Faber, 1940. An excellent and scholarly book. Fascinating reading for any civilized reader.

[187]

Index

INDEX